CONTENTS

This book is dedicated to my husband, Chris, my stepdaughters, Kylee and Hayley, to my parents, Marilyn and Mike Slagle, and to the many stepfamilies I've had the privilege of working with during the past 14 years.

INTRODUCTION

Being a stepparent is hard enough, even on the easy days. Take heart, no matter if you've been together for one year or 41 years, stepparenting is challenging for everyone. If you're currently wondering if being in a blended family is worth it, if you are considering leaving or divorcing your partner due to challenges with your children, or even if things are going ok for you, this workbook will support you on your journey to better communication, cooperation, and commitment.

No two step-parenting situations are exactly alike, from the reasons we become stepparents, to the situations we're dealing with, each of our experiences is unique. However, each blended family has shared experiences and the stages of stepparenting generally follow a similar pattern. We meet and fall in love with our partner, meet their children, commit to a long-term relationship, and then co-parenting issues begin. On average, it takes seven years to successfully blend a family, and there are many predictable and frustrating issues along the way.

Becoming engaged to my husband, Chris, was one of the happiest times in my life. I was thrilled that not only I had found the person I wanted to spend the rest of my life loving every single day, but I also adored his two little girls (then 3 and 5) and couldn't wait for us to become a family! Chris and I have now been married for over a decade and I love him more now than I ever thought possible. However, we have had some really tough moments as we learned how to blend our family. I admit, there were times I had to make a conscious decision whether or not I wanted to fight for our relationship and none of this was made easier because of the dynamics involving his girls and his sometimes difficult-to-work-with ex. When you become a stepparent, chances are the ex will always be there, reminding both you and your partner of their past: bad relationship decisions, bad habits, disagreements, and mistakes they may have made while raising their children, etc. You may believe your life and your marriage would be perfect without that one little (or not so little) hiccup.

Nobody understands the challenges of step-parenting like a fellow stepparent. I have been through the good and the challenging, the joy and intense feelings of frustration and overwhelm, and quite honestly there have been times I was ready to walk away. I understand how hard marriage can be, and then, when you add the additional challenge of step-parenting, well it's quite the wild ride! For the past several years, I have coached stepparents on how to handle their challenges and have witnessed firsthand many of the common issues that stepparents encounter. I have learned that stepparents, like everyone else, create many of our own problems, but that is the good news because it gives us the power to solve our own problems!

This workbook is designed for stepparents to work through so they can learn how to improve their relationships and increase their happiness in their family. Each chapter will help you to work through life's challenges and frustrations, so you can become stronger as a couple. As you complete this workbook, you will learn to communicate more effectively, work better with your partner as a team, learn how to prioritize your relationship, and become better co-parents (even when a hostile co-parent is involved). The assignments at the end of each chapter are the key to making the changes you long to create! So, make sure you complete each assignment and try to discuss them with your partner. You can go through the workbook in any order, however, I strongly encourage you to complete the assignments prior to moving on to the next chapter.

Are you ready for a change? Let's go!

ASSIGNMENT 1

In the box below, write down a list of the things you love and appreciate about your partner. Share this list with them, and keep it for later when things get difficult with the ex or with your partner.

ASSIGNMENT 2

In the box below, write down goals you have for your relationship, for yourselves, and for your family. Keep in mind the key to creating effective goals: **SMART**

Specific	**S**imple	**S**ensible
Measurable	**M**eaningful	**M**otivating
Achievable	**A**ttainable	**A**ppropriate
Relevant	**R**easonable	**R**esults-based
Timely	**T**ime-Bound	**T**rackable

ASSIGNMENT 3

In the box below, list any obstacles that could happen, or have happened, to derail you from achieving the goals you listed above. Possibilities include custody battles, child support, inappropriate boundaries with a co-parent, issues with your stepchildren, etc.

CHAPTER 1

My Philosophical Approach To Step-Parenting

The Only Person You Have the Power To Change Is YOU!

Each of us begins our journey as a stepparent with various lessons we have learned throughout our lives. A few of us start our new role as stepparents with a healthy mindset, a positive relationship with our partner's ex, and a firm foundation of parenting and coping skills to help us through the ups and downs of life as a stepparent. However, most of us begin our journey into step-parenting, stumbling in the dark. We struggle to gain footing, direction, and purpose like a treasure hunter without a map, compass, or innate sense of direction. Fortunately for you, I have created a map to help you understand where to go on your journey as a stepparent, and as you complete the assignments in this workbook, you'll be forming your compass to help you find your way.

The first and most important lesson that I have to teach you is that you are the only person you have the power to change! We all have life experiences and beliefs that cause us to have strong, uncomfortable emotional reactions; however, there are times when our interpretations of situations are wrong and thus cause us more difficulty in our relationships. When these experiences occur, often, we do not know how to best deal with our emotions, which is partially due to a lack of social/emotional skills. As a coach and moderator in online step-parenting support groups, I've seen how stepparents create or exacerbate problems because of how we interpret and react to life experiences, especially when they involve our stepchildren's biological parents.

Social/emotional skills include: coping strategies, recognizing thinking errors, identifying cognitive bias and not making assumptions based on cognitive bias, taking time to stop and think before reacting, etc. It's not necessarily your fault if you lack practical coping skills because they are generally not taught in our families, schools, or culture. However, you wish to be a successful and happy parent or stepparent, so you MUST learn how to deal with your emotions and be proactive, rather than reactive, in difficult situations, and this means you must learn coping skills.

The human brain naturally assigns a meaning, purpose, and lesson/reason for each of our life experiences. Most "meaning-making" occurs within our subconscious mind. Our subconscious uses past experiences and our deeply ingrained beliefs (both negative and positive) to determine how we feel and act. To discontinue negative responses, we must begin to recognize our subconscious thoughts and how we interpret life's interactions. We will continue to act out the same negative behaviors, patterns, and reactions until we do so.

For example, most people fear or believe they're not "good enough." When we think we're not good enough, we look for evidence to confirm that belief. So, suppose a biological parent (we'll call them your co-parent in this workbook) or your stepchildren say or do something negative to/about you. In that case, you will interpret it as confirmation that they believe that you are not good enough. You feel frustrated, angry, and hurt. Your internal dialogue confirms your subconscious belief and stores it away for future proof that you are not good enough. This reaction isn't caused by your co-parent or stepchildren thinking you are not good enough - your own negative thinking patterns cause this reaction. You believe you are not good enough.

Becoming aware of and changing your thoughts and beliefs is a foundational skill learned in cognitive-behavioral therapy. The goal of cognitive-behavioral therapy is to help you become aware of your negative thinking patterns to change your thoughts and behaviors. When you begin to become aware of how you're interpreting certain situations, you can decide if your interpretation is correct, if you care what your co-parent or stepchildren think, and what you want to do about it. When you recognize and change your thoughts, your behaviors also change. When you react without being aware that one of your negative beliefs is triggered, your reaction may complicate or escalate the situation.

For example, early in my marriage, before I understood my subconscious negative beliefs, my co-parent would text my husband late at night to change my stepdaughters' pickup plans, and I would become upset. My assumption/interpretation was that she was giving us late notice on purpose to mess with us, that she didn't care about the girls' or our time, and that she was purposely trying to make our lives harder, and so on. The truth is, she likely wasn't even thinking of us. She was doing what worked best for her. Even if she were intentionally behaving to slight us, nothing I could have said or done would have made her care about how her actions affected us.

My old subconscious belief was, "people have to like me for me to be a good person," and I wanted to prove to her I was good. I wanted her to respect me. I didn't realize until I examined my thoughts that how she feels about me reflects who she is, not who I am, and what she thinks of me is none of my business. When I let go of what I perceived as the way she thought of me and stopped personalizing what she did, and when I realized I am a good person, regardless of what she thinks, I became much happier and less reactive.

Hopefully, this example helps you understand what I mean about becoming aware of our subconscious thoughts and interpretations and deciding whether they work for or against us. I take all my coaching clients through exercises designed to help identify subconscious thoughts. We become powerful when we learn how to recognize and then work to change our untrue/negative subconscious beliefs.

Recognizing and changing our thought patterns is achieved through mindful observation. When we practice mindful observation, we notice our thoughts out of curiosity, and in a state of neutrality, like a scientist. Here is how it works. We have a thought, such as "My co-parent is trying to create drama in my partnership because they hate me." We notice the thought, and from a place of neutrality, we assess it, "Hmm, that is interesting. Why am I thinking this way?" Then we get to decide whether that thought is working for us or working against us, and whether or not we want to keep believing it. This process can be complex because, as meaning-making machines, we all try to make sense out of this business of life, and sometimes we get it wrong, and that's ok. Becoming perfect isn't the goal of mindfulness - the goal is becoming aware.

ASSIGNMENT 1

Use the box below to answer. What fears do you have about being a stepparent? What do you love about being a parent or stepparent?

ASSIGNMENT 2

In the box below write down your thoughts/beliefs you have about being a stepparent.

ASSIGNMENT 3

Think about the way you respond when someone upsets you. What thoughts do you have? What feelings do you have? Do you think they're trying to hurt you, or they're doing it intentionally? How do you act? Write your answers in the box below

ASSIGNMENT 4

As you think about the responses you recorded in Assignment 3, decide if your response in these situations is helping or hurting your relationships. Is your interpretation of situations and your reaction to them making you happy? Is it making your relationships better? If not, write down what you want to try differently, use the box below.

ASSIGNMENT 5

How do you see your reactions impacting your relationship with your stepchildren? How about your partner? And your co-parent? Write your answers in the box below.

CHAPTER 2

Mindset And Subconscious Programming

The Importance Of Mindset

How you interpret life's situations, how you feel, and how you choose to react; all of these things contribute to how successfully or unsuccessfully you handle the challenges that step-parenting can throw your way. Your thoughts and beliefs are part of your subconscious programming, and they contribute to how you see the world around you and how you react to it, creating a pattern of behavior or habits. These thoughts and beliefs make up what we call mindset, and the outcome of your life's goals and relationships largely depends upon your mindset.

Mindset develops in early childhood and continues to change well into our young adult lives. When we are young, we learn how to interpret the world around us by observing and mimicking our parents' and caregivers' behaviors, beliefs, and actions. Each time we behave in a way that creates our desired outcome (love, affection, food, etc.), our subconscious stores away that behavior, thought, or emotional response in the "it worked" category. Like a computer, our subconscious works automatically, running these stored programs to serve a purpose, and our brains' primary purpose is our survival.

Survival programming happens in the limbic system, buried deep within our cerebral cortex. The limbic system is exceptionally efficient, choosing only the programs that have proven successful in the past, regardless of new information that we might take in. These set programs make it difficult, but not impossible, to change our mindset because from our limbic system's perspective, the things we believe, feel, and do have kept us alive. Our brain loves to be alive and operates in a way to keep us alive! Only through conscious, consistent effort can we adjust our mindset and subconscious thoughts, and by so doing, transform our behavior to change our lives.

Let us examine the example of a scarcity mindset and how it might have become programmed in your limbic system. As a child, you heard the phrase "Money doesn't grow on trees" when you asked your parents for something you wanted. The subtle messages your parents sent you about money created a scarcity mindset in your subconscious, which said, "Money does not grow on trees; therefore, money is difficult to obtain." Perhaps your subconscious took this belief even further "Money does not grow on trees; therefore money is difficult to obtain, and I am not worth the effort." This scarcity mindset creates a pattern of beliefs and behaviors about making and spending money that will continue to harm you as an adult.

Another way that our brain receives subconscious programming is by observing the behavior of someone in a position of authority over us, usually our parents. Unfortunately, when we are children, we cannot distinguish between fact and fiction in what we observe - is what I'm seeing accurate or simply a person's beliefs? We have no filter for our parents' behaviors, and what our parents believe, do, and say is passed on to us; it becomes our subconscious programming.

Perhaps your parents had a difficult relationship when you were a child, and you heard or observed them in repeated conflicts. You learned from the way they successfully or unsuccessfully resolved disagreements. In this example, a subconscious belief that all marriages or relationships are complicated or contentious subtly encourages you to create or submit to a pattern of conflict in your key relationships. It might seem overwhelming when you think of the generations of families passing on unhealthy subconscious beliefs and behaviors. However, the good news in this is that you have the power to change your subconscious programming and thus change your conscious thoughts and mindset.

Changing our mindset is simple but not easy. When our brain runs subconscious programming (e.g., "I'm not good enough," "nobody loves me") for long enough, it builds up a powerful, quick neural pathway from external stimuli/triggers to your limbic system. Your brain builds these superfast pathways to conserve energy because it perceives everything as a threat to your life, and it cannot distinguish between an actual threat, like coming across a bear when you're hiking, and a psychological threat, like dealing with a manipulative co-parent. Even though high-conflict co-parents definitely create stressful interactions, our physical safety isn't in danger in most cases. When we remember that our lives are not in danger and we are in control of our behavior, we are empowered to choose to use coping strategies to help us calm down and interact in a more positive way; this is what it means to retrain your brain to be proactive instead of reactive.

How to Change Your Mindset

Changing your mindset takes conscious, consistent effort. The first step is recognizing, acknowledging, and tracking your thoughts as different situations arise. You may think you don't have automatic assumptions or negative thoughts, but unless you've done some intense therapy or inner-work, I promise you, they're in there. Even if you have done extensive therapy or intense inner-work, you will still have negative thoughts and self-talk that you will benefit from recognizing and changing.

Our automatic thoughts are called self-talk, and studies have shown that between 70-90% of our daily self-talk is negative. Negative self-talk might sound like "Nobody likes me" or "I'm such an idiot," or "I can't do that," or "I'll never understand XYZ…", and so on. Unsurprisingly, after thinking negative thoughts all day, we don't feel good about ourselves or our ability to complete challenging tasks, including negotiating a compromise with a hostile co-parent. We want to give up on even trying and instead indulge in comforting activities like laying in bed and eating ice cream all day. (Not that I'm judging you, ice cream is yummy!)

Mindset falls into two categories: growth mindset or fixed mindset. A growth mindset includes positive beliefs that we can become better with work, dedication, or commitment. A growth mindset chooses to look for positive lessons or outcomes from life's challenges.

A fixed mindset means that we think that life will never get any better than it already is and that it isn't worth trying because nothing ever works out for us. A fixed mindset means that you don't have the will or the desire to make positive changes in your life because you don't believe they will make any difference.

A growth mindset thought may sound like, "I can go to counseling and work on this issue, I can make positive changes in my life" versus a fixed mindset, "Well, this is just who I am, and I can't change it." The quickest and easiest way to get your brain to become growth mindset oriented is to add "yet" to your sentences. "Yet" changes "I can't do that" to "I can't do that yet."

If you want to read more about growth and fixed mindsets, I highly recommend Carol Dweck's book, *Mindset: The New Psychology of Success.*

ASSIGNMENT 1

Get a notebook or journal and carry it around with you for 3-5 days. Write down any thoughts or self-talk you notice.

Common Thinking Errors

The exercise above, which allows you to objectively observe and document your automatic negative thought patterns, which I call thinking errors, is the first step in changing your mindset. Like a computer's programming glitch, thinking errors cause undesirable behaviors. They are more likely to manifest when we experience intense emotions, during times of stress, or when we are struggling in our relationships. Thinking errors can also display when we enjoy a period of peace, increased security, relationship progress, or affluence. Most thinking errors are irrational and inaccurate, and we all have them. If you want more information on thinking errors, you can find it through a quick online search using terms like "thinking errors," "cognitive distortions," or "automatic negative thoughts."

Some of the most common thinking errors are listed below, which is by no means an exhaustive list, but it will help you begin to identify some of your thinking errors.

- Filtering out the positive—focusing only on the negative parts of relationships or situations.
- Binocular vision or minimizing/catastrophizing—making an issue more significant than it is, OR not taking a problem seriously enough.
- Black and white thinking—thinking about situations in extreme ways. Someone who thinks in black & white will commonly use the words "never" or "always," "best" or "worst," "good" or "bad" to describe their emotions or situations. For example, "You never listen." or "I'm always the bad guy." The current political climate in the United States is an illustrative example of black & white thinking.
- Fortune telling—trying to predict the future without enough information. In a step-parenting situation, this might sound like "I know that (the co-parent) is going to cause drama this weekend at the drop-off." They might cause drama, but we never know for sure what's going to happen.
- Mind reading—assuming you know what someone else is thinking. E.g., "You're just trying to make me mad."
- Emotional reasoning—believing our emotions are rational or factual. We may think, "I feel like an idiot, so I must be an idiot." Our thoughts and feelings are not facts; they're just thoughts and feelings that may have truthful elements, but we need to look at them individually to decide.
- Making it personal—blaming ourselves for things that are not our fault. This thinking error is widespread among children whose parents are divorced; they blame themselves for their parent's divorce.
- Blame game—blaming others for things that are our responsibility or assigning blame or fault when uncomfortable situations arise. No one wins the blame game.
- Personalization—believing that other people do things because of us. For example, if your stepchildren don't want to come over one night, you may think, "They just don't want to see me."
- Idealization—holding ourselves or relationships to an unrealistic ideal or standard. For example, if you compare your relationship to an influencer or friend's social media posts.
- Perfectionism—thinking that you have to be perfect or you're worthless.
- Should statements—believing or telling yourself that things "should" be a certain way. For example, "I should love my stepchildren like my own," or "I should give up my free time when my stepchildren are here."

How to Change Thinking Errors By Reframing

Once we identify our common thinking errors, we are empowered because we can use a technique to correct them called reframing. It is important to note that not all negative thoughts are thinking errors. For example, I may say to myself, "I'll never play professional baseball," which is accurate for a woman in her mid 40's who is lucky to hit a softball when at-bat. Sometimes we have negative beliefs that are accurate, but it's just as important to reframe those types of thoughts when they harm our mental health. In this example, I could reframe saying, "I'll never play professional baseball, but I enjoy playing on my community softball team."

Here is an example of reframing a common thinking error most stepparents experience.
1. Identify the negative thought.
2. Identify the thinking error and become intentional about stopping the pattern.
3. Look for evidence that supports the opposite of the belief. Ask yourself if the thought is realistic, accurate, or harmful.
4. Replace it with a positive thought or truth, or add the word "yet."

Negative Thought	Identify the Thinking Error	Ask, "Is it true?" Look for evidence it is not true.	Replace the negative thought with a positive one, or add the word "Yet."
I'm not going to pick up my stepchildren this weekend. My co-parent hates me.	Mind reading	It might be true. My co-parent looks at me like they don't like me. My co-parent doesn't talk to me much, but they told me "thank you" for buying the kids new winter coats and boots last week.	I don't want to go to pick up my stepchildren this weekend. Being around my co-parent feels uncomfortable. My co-parent isn't always friendly, but I will go with my partner to pick up their childrn this weekend. I love to be with the children and let them know they're important to me.

Intentional Gratitude Practice

Another way we can reframe negative thoughts and improve our mindset is through an intentional gratitude practice. Practicing gratitude has been shown to improve relationships, physical and mental health, increase self-esteem, enhance empathy, provide a better quality of sleep, and increase mental resilience to help you rebound from difficult situations. Gratitude is a simple daily practice that can make your life significantly better, and by being grateful, you can shift yourself out of negative self-talk.

Intentionally practicing gratitude can be accomplished in several ways:
- Keep a gratitude journal. Create a list of three things you're grateful for every day. Challenge yourself to list new things each day and get creative.
- Openly express to your partner what you're grateful for, use the words "I appreciate you because…" frequently.
- Notice and appreciate the good things in life and the world around you. Take time to enjoy nature, people, music, art, etc.
- Make a gratitude jar or box. Create a container and list items on slips of paper that you are grateful for, then read one every morning to remind yourself to look for the positive.
- Create a family gratitude tree, a fun activity during Thanksgiving. Use a natural branch or a picture of a tree mounted on the refrigerator or wall, cut out leaves, have your family write things they are grateful for, and tie or glue them to your gratitude tree.
- Purchase a ready-made Gratitude Journal or subscribe to a daily gratitude prompt to help you journal thoughts such as: "I'm grateful for these three things I can touch."

It takes time, patience, and courage to recognize and reframe your thinking errors; please don't get discouraged. As a school psychologist, I have taught this process of identifying and changing thinking errors many times to large groups. Only after repeatedly teaching about this concept and identifying my thinking errors has this process become automatic, as long as I am mindful and not distracted. And now, after years of practice, I have finally started to observe my thinking errors without judgment. It is only from a place of neutrality that I can reframe them into thoughts that work for my benefit. If I can do this, you can too!

ASSIGNMENT 2

Look over the list of thinking errors and decide which you tend to use most frequently. Keep track of how many times you use those over the next week, use the box below.

ASSIGNMENT 3

Look at the list of thinking errors and notice which one/ones your partner uses most frequently. DO NOT TALK TO THEM ABOUT THIS YET. Also, don't write these down because I don't want you to fixate on your partner using these thinking errors. Notice which thinking errors your children/stepchildren uses the most. Notice which thinking errors your parents use the most. Pay attention to thinking errors everywhere you go and with everyone you talk to, but don't talk to anyone about it yet because people around you may not know about them and may perceive this as criticism.

ASSIGNMENT 4

As you notice which thinking errors you and your partner use the most often, mentally ask yourself if what you and your partner are saying is true. Is it true that you can't do something in your life? Is it true that things never work out for you? Is it true that if your co-parent weren't in your life that everything would be sunshine and rainbows?

ASSIGNMENT 5

As you start to notice which thinking errors you use most frequently and how they sound in your head, reframe them. Use the table below to reframe your most common negative thoughts and their corresponding thinking errors.

Table To Reframe Negative Thoughts and Thinking Errors

Negative Thought	Identify the Thinking Error	Ask, "Is it true?" Look for evidence it is not true.	Replace the negative thought with a positive one, or add the word "Yet."

ASSIGNMENT 6

Talk to your partner about thinking errors. Have them identify which ones they use most frequently. Ask them if they would be interested in working on reframing them. Journal your thoughts below.

The Illusion of Control

We all have someone in our life who likes to be in control of everything and everyone. Is it your boss, a coworker, a parent, a sibling, or a relative? Is it you? (It was totally me!) Whomever this person is, they're not likely to be very happy. The more we try to control things, the more unhappy we become when we realize certain circumstances and people are out of our control.

Control is an Illusion

The only thing we will ever really have control over is ourselves. Let me repeat that. The only person you can control is you. The only behavior you can control is yours. The only thoughts you can control are yours. The only actions you can control, you guessed it, are yours. Even when we begin learning how to take charge of our lives, we often recognize we don't control every aspect of our own lives. The illusion of control, or the need to control every part of our lives, directly results from thinking errors.

It takes time, practice, and discipline to get to the point where you can manage your emotions, be proactive rather than reactive, recognize your thinking errors, and make the best choices you can. At the root of many high emotion conflicts in step-parenting is control. We create unnecessary conflicts when we try to control our co-parents, partners, stepchildren, or circumstances instead of healthily controlling our emotions.

Generally speaking, in U.S. culture, we have difficulty with emotional literacy. Emotional literacy is the ability to put thoughts and feelings into words so you can understand and interact with others in a more effective way. Our culture likes to buffer or stuff our emotions, choosing to ignore what is happening inside our heads and hearts rather than facing our emotional conflicts head-on. We also tend to lash out in anger when we have a difficult interaction; this is especially true when we don't know how to manage our emotions or replace our uncomfortable feelings with more comfortable thinking errors. When we increase our emotional literacy and let go of control, we empower ourselves to change. I always tell people I'm a recovering perfectionist and control freak; if I can change for the better, so can you!

Most efforts to control a situation are rooted in anxiety or fear: not knowing what to expect from someone, knowing and dreading what to expect from them, fearing the worst will happen, and so on. Step-parenting especially causes anxiety because we never know what to expect from our stepchildren or co-parent, so our limbic system perceives every interaction as a threat. The irony of the illusion of control is that the more we try to control our others, the more out of control we become. When you focus on yourself and learn to manage your emotions, you discover that you don't need everything to exactly go as you plan because you know that you can handle whatever happens. Conversely, when you can't or don't exert self-control, interactions or everyday occurrences in your life can quickly escalate into conflict.

Giving up the illusion of control allows you space to exercise faith in God, the Universe, or your

Higher Power in whatever form it takes. Releasing the illusion of control also allows you to reflect on the person you want to be, your highest self, and act accordingly. When we relinquish the need to control everything that happens in our lives, the door to opportunity opens, and you will find the experiences you need to become your best self. And finally, when we give up our need to control, we experience freedom in every way. Giving up the illusion of control won't change how your co-parent acts, but that's not why you do it; we give up control to free ourselves from reacting to others' actions and empower ourselves to act in a way that helps us find peace.

ASSIGNMENT 7

Are there areas or people in your life that you try to control? What/who are they? Write a list below, focusing on what you feel you must control and the things/situations you like to control.

ASSIGNMENT 8

Which items on your list are related to your life as a stepparent? Co-parenting?

ASSIGNMENT 9

If you could learn to give up the illusion of control, what would that make room for in your life? Journal your thoughts below.

ASSIGNMENT 10

Fill out the blank chart below with what you can and can't control in your life. The next page provides an example.

WHAT I CAN'T CONTROL

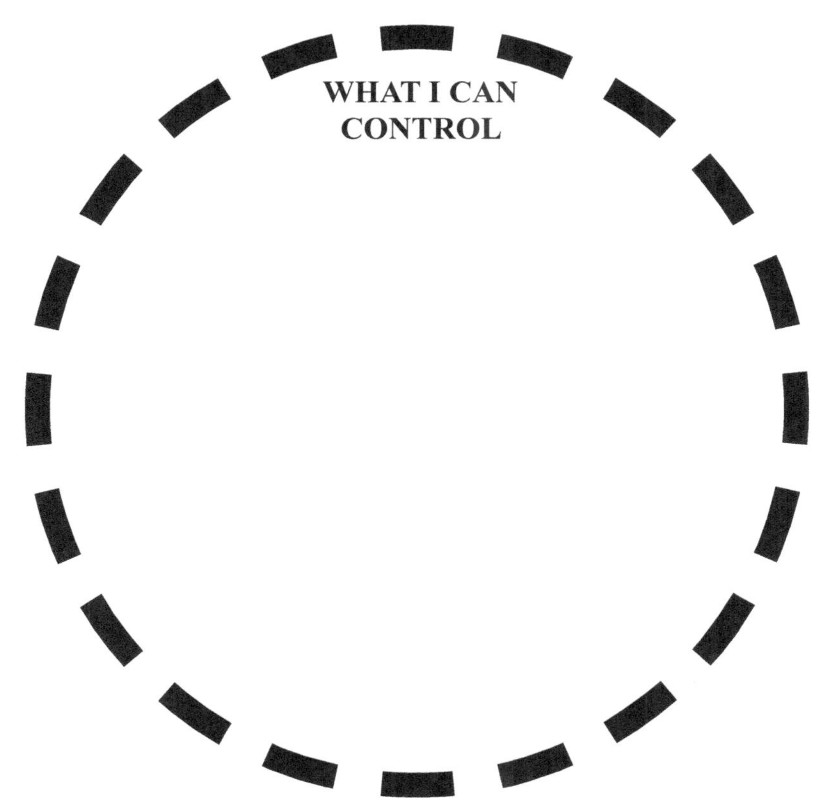

WHAT I CAN'T CONTROL
Someone else's decisions
Co-parent
How others treat me
Child support
WHAT I CAN CONTROL
My response to my challenges
How I respond to others
Being kind
My own happiness
Court
Asking for help
Trying again
Who likes me
Being honest
Taking care of myself
My decisions
Forgiving
How I spend my free time
Others being honest
Who loves me
If someone else keeps trying
Others forgiving me

CHAPTER 3

The Only Person You Have The Power to Change is You!

Create Flow In Life By Focusing On Your Well-Being

In my work as a school psychologist, we have a saying: "Where attention goes, behavior grows." Our happiness as stepparents, as in life, is directly related to where we place our focus. When we focus on things we cannot control, our lives become more difficult. Chapter Two discussed how control is an illusion and how your thoughts and behaviors are the only things you can truly control. This chapter will discuss how to make the changes necessary to have a happier life, which will help you become a more effective, happier stepparent.

Focusing on your well-being means:
- You remember and nurture who you are
- You acknowledge and fulfill your individual needs
- You have a life outside of your parental roles which brings you happiness and fulfillment
- You understand that the other roles you play are just as important and valid as your role as a stepparent

It's so easy for us to hyperfocus on parenting. The process of finding our groove in life is ongoing and requires a lot of flexibility, patience, and time. Focusing on yourself and your own well-being does not mean you become self-centered, it means you focus on making changes in your mindset and emotional literacy, and letting go of the things you cannot control to return the focus on the things that you can, which means you.

There is a common myth that we can create balance in our lives, that is all it is, a myth. Imagine standing in a circle, plates surrounding you, all spinning on poles. Each of these plates is one role you play, or one area in your life: Work, Partner, Stepparent, Friend, etc. When we hyperfocus on only one role and try to exert complete control there, the rest of the plates destabilize, stress builds up, we become unhappy and forget what's important to us. Our entire life is reduced to catching the falling plates or cleaning up the mess when they finally crash down to the ground.

When we focus on what we can change, we devote part of our attention to all of the roles we choose to take on and keep those plates spinning, creating flow, which allows us to have happier, more stable relationships. Balance is a myth because it implies that once balanced, all your plates will spin effortlessly, which they won't. Inevitably one plate will start to slow, creating a little wobble. When this happens, if we are centered, we detect the wobble before it becomes a big problem and address it in a proactive rather than reactive way. Our plates keep spinning, messes are far and few between, and much easier to clean up.

Focus On The Positive

When we focus mainly on problems, we create unnecessary drama, and daily life struggles become more significant. When we engage in hyper-critical behavior, we lose sight of the good in our relationships, especially in stepparenting and marriage. When I focus on things that my stepchildren or husband are (or are not) doing or the drama that my co-parent creates, that becomes all I can see. I lose my focus (and my cool) and give them the power to control me. I don't know about you, but I don't want my co-parent, my husband, or my stepchildren to have power over my happiness at all!

When you focus on yourself, you're choosing to focus on solutions rather than problems. Instead of focusing on the things other people are doing that I don't like, something that irritates me, or that I dislike about my co-parent's actions, I shift my focus to my thoughts, feelings, beliefs, and actions. Doing this helps me disengage from problems and come up with solutions.

To disengage means to use pre-planned coping strategies to separate our self-worth and happiness from any given conflict. When we disengage, we can create distance between our happiness and the outcome of the obstacles we encounter. In this way, we become proactive instead of reactive. Disengagement does not mean buffering or stuffing your emotions; it does not mean becoming numb or distant. It means you understand that your intrinsic self-worth and happiness do not depend on the outcome of a conflict, and you act accordingly. It also means that you allow yourself to feel and process through the emotions of conflicts.

When I disengage, instead of focusing on what I do not want in my life, I ask myself: What are my goals? What are my dreams? How can I work towards those? What kind of partner do I want to be? What type of stepparent do I want to be? Disengagement means choosing the actions that empower you to become the man or woman you want to be, no matter how difficult the journey is.

As a school psychologist, I've spent most of my time in middle schools (grades 7-9). Do you remember your middle school experiences? Most adults agree these awkward years are torturous, and even those who were popular or enjoyed middle school would never willingly go back. The way some co-parents behave reminds me a lot of what I see in middle school: tons of drama, instigating to get a response, and many struggles to disengage. Sometimes people do not disengage because they just don't know how; sometimes, they lack emotional literacy and struggle to deal with conflict. Again, this isn't a judgment. I've often behaved like a middle schooler as a stepparent. Of all the students I counsel, those who make the most progress are the ones who are open to learning how to disengage from what's going around them and the issues that other people create. Like my students, as adults, when we focus on what is out of our control, we feel like our lives are out of control; we feel powerless, frustrated, and stuck, all of which diverts our focus from what we can change in our lives. If we want to progress and create the life we desire, we need to learn to disengage and refocus.

Focusing on yourself can be difficult and requires a lot of practice, especially when you have someone you feel is actively interfering in your life or making choices that negatively impact you and your family. So, how do you disengage from conflict, or drama, or hostile behavior from your partner, stepchildren, or co-parent?

Strategies For Disengagement

Disengagement takes positive action. When conflict arises, we become stressed. Doing something to destress at the moment is often not enough to keep you focused. Instead, we need to practice preventative and intervention strategies to redirect our attention to positive thoughts, emotions, and actions.

Preventative strategies include:
- Managing your self-talk by identifying thinking errors and creating a plan to reframe them when you notice them
- Identifying and becoming aware of your triggers and choosing to focus on something else when triggers occur
- Managing your emotions in a healthy way
- Doing fun things that make you happy
- Planning and participating in activities to help you relax and decrease your stress levels
- Practicing self-care regularly
- Recognizing that when people show you who they are, you must trust that they're acting in a way that is consistent with that
- Making a conscious decision to let their crap go because it's about them, not you

Intervention strategies can include:
- Putting the phone down and walking away when you're upset
- Taking a walk
- Forcing yourself to take five deep, slow breaths before you respond to conflict
- Listening to music that helps you feel and release your feelings
- Talking to a trusted friend
- Venting in a stepparent support group
- Sharing your feelings with your partner, being careful to avoid blame or shame
- Hiring a therapist to help you sort through your feelings

Of all the options above, I highly encourage you to see a therapist to help you analyze your feelings, learn coping techniques, identify healthy and unhealthy behaviors, and create individualized preventative and intervention strategies to help you disengage in your conflicts. Even though I am a school psychologist who practices counseling every day, as I've gone through the struggles of adjusting to stepparenting, seeing a therapist has made a tremendous impact for good in my life. I highly recommend it to my stepparent friends and clients.

Another way we can disengage is to participate in private or group coaching. In my private coaching practice, Step Up Mentoring, I help you in your role as a stepparent to find greater peace and fulfillment by understanding how your expectations are hurting you and your relationships. During our coaching sessions, I help you learn how to handle common stepparent triggers and set reasonable goals for your relationships. I also guide you as you learn how to heal old wounds and let go of hurts impacting your relationships. Finally, I help you find support from other stepparents who understand what they're going through. Suppose you wish to speak to me about how private coaching might help you in your life as a stepparent. In that case, you can contact me at sara@sarasusov.com or on my website, www.sarasusov.com, which includes information about the different options for available coaching courses.

ASSIGNMENT 1

Think about your primary focus. Are most of the things you're focused on things you can or cannot control? You can use the diagram from the last page in Chapter Two to remind you. Using the box below, journal how you feel about where you focus most of your time and energy.

ASSIGNMENT 2

Where do you want to spend your time and energy? Where would you like your focus to be? What is most important to you? Write the answers below.

ASSIGNMENT 3

Pay attention to your thoughts and feelings; notice whether you're thinking about the past, present, or future. Try to bring your mind into the present. Pay attention to how it feels to focus on what's happening right now - use the box below and journal how you feel when you are present in your thoughts.

Find Your Passion and Purpose

When we learn how to create a happier, more fulfilling life, we often talk about finding our passion and life purpose. If you are new to this concept, it might feel superficial or selfish because many of us genuinely find happiness and fulfillment in our role as stepparents. We wonder if we are egocentric by pursuing other interests outside of our family. However, when you devote time to your hobbies, passions, or purpose, it is anything but selfish because it helps you to find more joy and fulfillment in life, thus making you a happier, more joyful caregiver.

So, what are your passions? Maybe you are passionate about exercise, traveling, doing crafts, riding horses, working with animals, participating in religious or spiritual practices, helping other people, art, or music? Maybe you are passionate about books, learning, or gaming? When trying to discover your passions in life, don't look for a lightbulb "Ah-Ha!" moment; just write a list of things that you love to do and do those things. Or, maybe you don't have anything currently in your life that lights you up; in this case, write a list of things you might enjoy or would like to learn and begin there.

Your passion and your purpose are usually two different things. Travel is one of my passions, but I don't feel like it's my purpose in life. I love animals and have a passion for my dogs, too, but again, however much I love my dogs, they're not my purpose in life. If you're not sure of your life's purpose, that's okay. Sometimes we need time, experimentation, and experiences to find our purpose.

Purpose does not need to be some grand mission and most often is not what you do for a career. Some people I know feel their purpose is to become incredible stepparents. Others think their purpose is to love and help people feel loved and cheer them on as they work towards reaching their potential. Some people find their purpose as healers, writers, or mentors. Many people are passionate about and find their purpose in leaving a mark on the world by building a successful business. Whatever you decide your purpose is, know that it is okay to have your purpose change throughout your life. The point isn't fulfilling some predetermined path or destiny; the objective is to bring meaning and happiness into your life, keep you focused on your goals, and become a better, happier person.

Dealing With Discouragement

Discouragement can set in when we hit "mid-life" and look back at what we have accomplished and wonder if it was worthwhile. Many of us follow a typical life pattern when we reach young adulthood and go to college or find some type of career training, which leads to a job or a career that we may or may not love. We fall in love, enter into a relationship, become committed, have a family, and then they grow up, leave home, and then what? Remember that there is so much time between young adulthood and our golden years, and there are so many amazing things we can accomplish, both as stepparents and as individuals. Please don't give up on your dreams just because they haven't happened yet. This planet needs you and your gifts, and it needs to be your best self. Without taking time to tap into who you are and what lights you up, you're not really living. You're just existing.

ASSIGNMENT 4

Do something that you love this week, or try something new that you've wanted to try. What did you like about it? How did it feel? Write your answers in the box below.

ASSIGNMENT 5

Try to find a quiet space for 5–10 minutes for you to contemplate what you want to accomplish in your life. It's a good idea to write a list of goals, or a bucket list, for the next 1, 3, 5, 10, and 20 years of your life. Write down some of the highlights here.

Self-care

Step-parenting is hard work! Raising children is a perilous adventure, to say the least. Still, when you throw in the other challenges stepparents face, like high-conflict co-parents, court battles, hostility from the ex, disrespect from your stepchildren, resistance to your authority, "You're not my real mom/dad," etc., life can become extremely heavy and draining. None of us grew up thinking that being a stepparent was our ultimate goal. But here we are, trying our best to blend a family in love and unity, and it is exhausting; emotionally, physically, and mentally. As a stepparent, taking care of your health, mental and physical, is of utmost importance.

Self-care is a big buzzword right now, and a lot of people think it means getting a massage, taking a bubble bath, or getting your nails done, but it's so much more than that! Going to therapy or working with a life coach/mentor is self-care. So is setting healthy boundaries, taking a break from family and home life when you need it, or having your partner share responsibilities for discipline, school, chores, etc. Self-care can also be doing things that enrich your life, like reading good books, listening to podcasts, or going to retreats. Any activity that helps with your physical, mental, or emotional well-being can be classified as self-care and will reduce stress and anxiety, and help improve your relationships. Personally, my favorite self-care activities include seeing my therapist, frequent meditation, mindfulness practices, and exercise, as well as hiring mentors/life coaches.

For example, I've let go of my expectations through meditation and mindfulness practices and reduced my overall stress levels. Here is a list of some of meditation and mindfulness practice benefits. In just five to ten minutes daily, this practice will help you:
- Destress by focusing on breathing and the present moment
- Let go of the illusion of control
- When you increase your ability to tap into mindfulness, you gain patience
- Mindfulness helps you let go of judgments of yourself, your partner, stepchildren, and co-parent.

One of the reasons people skip self-care is because they think they cannot afford it or don't have the time to stop and take care of themselves. Our modern life moves at a faster pace than at any other time in history. We have higher rates of inflation and higher housing prices, which means most families need both parents to work at least one job to make ends meet. There is significant pressure for our children to participate in extra-curricular activities, which means more travel after school and late nights doing homework. In social media and our career cultures, we are constantly bombarded by words like "Hustle" and feel the need to stay busy because busyness is perceived as a measure of success. Soon, the pressure to do more and be more becomes wholly overwhelming, and we find ourselves crashing. Now, more than ever, we desperately need to take time to slow down and take care of ourselves. Whether you feel like you don't have the time or money to do it, self-care is critical, and the need for good self-care cannot be overstated when you are a stepparent. It isn't selfish to love yourself, take care of yourself, and make your happiness a priority; it's a necessity!

As with any new habit, consistency in self-care may be difficult. To get the most out of self-care, make a plan and set aside time when there will be no interruptions. Choose activities that you are most likely to enjoy so you will look forward to your self-care time and are less likely to set it aside. Try including the occasional activity with friends outside of your relationship. Have an accountability partner, pay for classes upfront, or schedule in advance, so you are more likely to follow through on your self-care commitments. Most of all, have fun and enjoy the time you spend taking care of yourself. YOU ARE WORTH IT!

ASSIGNMENT 6

Look at the self-care checklist in the appendices. Choose one activity you want to do daily or at least three times this week. Use the box below, write down what you're going to do and when you're going to do it.

ASSIGNMENT 7

Think about things that usually get in the way of your self-care. Write down what they are, along with a plan for how you're going to deal with them this week.

ASSIGNMENT 8

After you've finished your first week of self-care, write down how it went for you and what you want to change or add next week. Use the box below.

CHAPTER 4

Your Life As a Stepparent

Adjusting To Life In A Blended Family

You've probably heard that the first five years of marriage are the hardest. As newlyweds, you're learning how to share your space and time, adjusting to living with someone new, learning things you didn't know (and maybe don't really love) about your partner, altering your approach to finances, figuring out how to balance career and home, dealing with new in-laws, and many other changes. For 20% of couples in a first marriage, the marriage doesn't make it past five years. Unfortunately, current statistics for second marriages show they end in divorce 67% of the time, and third marriages end in divorce 74% of the time. When you consider the stressors that go into a second or third marriage, including co-parenting and blending families, these statistics probably don't surprise you.

For many couples in a first-time childless marriage, you have the luxury as a newlywed to learn how to adjust to marriage slowly by spending quality time together –just the two of you, experience and resolve conflict – between just the two of you, and learn life-love balance – just the two of you. All this changes when you marry someone who already has children. Suddenly you have to share your time and space not only with your partner but their children as well. When conflict arises, you may not want to fight in front of the children, so things can become strained between you and your partner when conflicts are unresolved. Your partner may feel that they have to choose between you and the children as they prioritize their time and energy, which is stressful for everyone involved. It becomes necessary to make plans around when the children will or will not be with you, and if you're doing fun things, it's hard to know the children might be missing out. Alternately, your partner may not want to do fun activities without their children, and you might feel like your life is on hold until the next time they come to your home.

Figuring out when or where to get intimate with your partner can also be tricky, depending on how often your stepchildren are with you and how comfortable you express your intimacy around them. In a blended family, you need to consider how you express physical intimacy, including cuddling, holding hands, or kissing, and if it will impact the children, and whether or not they will share what they see (and if you mind if they share) with the co-parent. When children see the intimacy between partners in a first marriage, it is just a normal part of their lives. Still, intimacy is just one more thing that you and your partner need to discuss in a second marriage.

The good news is that your marriage isn't doomed to fail - there are proven strategies that can help you be more successful and happy and increase your odds of staying together. Among these are: getting support through therapy or from a life coach, working to improve your communication, learning how to argue with your partner while staying connected emotionally, showing respect and consideration for your partner's feelings and opinions, and learning how to manage your emotions in a way that helps you.

When I married Chris, my emotional intelligence and ability to effectively handle situations were on the low-end of the spectrum. As a school psychologist, I frequently tell my students that most adults in my generation and my parent's generation did not learn social/emotional skills, which are critical in life and creating a happy marriage or any close relationship. I tell them that all children need to go to therapy because of things their parents did. It's not a matter of not if, but when and why therapy is necessary!

If we don't learn how to handle conflict in a constructive way or communicate to our partner what we need, our lives will be more difficult. You may feel like you don't know how to practice social/emotional skills. It can seem overwhelming, even though you know learning how to acknowledge, feel, and healthily deal with your emotions is critical to your happiness in marriage and your contentment with your life. Feeling like this is normal. It takes time and intentional practice to learn and to use these skills.

As you adjust to your new parenting situation, consider your needs and your partner's needs, as well as what your stepchildren need. Give yourself time and grace as you adjust. You will make mistakes. It's better to take your time to plan your approach rather than rush into it; this way, you will avoid making decisions in the heat of the moment when you may be under too much pressure to think quickly or make decisions when you're upset. The assignments in this chapter will help you decide with your partner how you want to parent and what your priorities and goals are for your stepchildren.

ASSIGNMENT 1

Write down and discuss with your partner what your expectations are and what issues you have had transitioning into co-parenting and step-parenting. Use the box below

ASSIGNMENT 2

Step back from your parenting role and look at how things are going. What is working for you, and what would you like to change? What do you need as you continue to adjust to the changing demands of blending a family?

ASSIGNMENT 3

Talk to your partner about going to individual or family therapy. Although you may not be having problems in your relationship, therapy can help improve your communication and help you deal with minor problems before they become unmanageable. Write down any issues you want to talk about here.

Married With (Their) Children

Chances are, when you fell in love with your partner, you knew there were children in their life. Maybe you have children of your own, and you understood what a parent's life looked like, or perhaps, like me, you didn't have children, and so you had an idea of what it means to be a parent, but not experience. When you're in a relationship with someone who has children, especially when the children are younger, the children have to come first sometimes, which means losing touch with each other can be easy.

In my experience, learning how to deal with children at the center of our lives was sometimes extremely difficult because I didn't know what to expect. When we met, Chris was still dealing with his family and marriage loss, and I didn't understand that. Before we were married, we didn't talk about the fact that sometimes the children had to come first. Since this is my first marriage, I wanted to have time with him as his first and only priority, which created unhappiness for both of us as we tried to figure out what worked for our family and our relationship.

As partners in a blended family, you can expect children to complicate your relationship, co-parenting or step-parenting, scheduling, and finances. The co-parent may be an emotionally healthy person who can co-parent effectively in the best-case scenario. In the worst-case scenario, they may be uninterested in the children, vindictive, or trying to hurt you through the children, creating even more significant difficulties while you're building your relationship with your partner. As a stepparent trying to develop a relationship with your stepchildren, "normal life" challenges like issues with your career, children's health, finances, and mental health can further complicate creating a happy blended family.

Marriage is difficult enough without the issues mentioned above. Add in the failure rate of second marriages and the factors that contribute to that, including exes and stepchildren, suddenly we realize how crucial it is that you find time to devote to building up yourself and your partner.

Your relationship must come first if you are to blend your family successfully. We will discuss making your relationship a priority in the next chapter. Suffice it to say that this will be a challenge, but I believe you are up for it!

Communicating Your Love

In his book The 5 Love Languages, Gary Chapman talks about five different ways people feel and express love: words of affirmation, gifts, acts of service, quality time, and physical touch. He theorizes that each of us has one primary love language, meaning that there is one way that people can behave towards us that feels most loving to us. We also have one secondary love language. Simply put, we do not all communicate our love in the same way, and we do not receive love in the same way. Your partner's love language matters! Watch how they express their love to others, which is a great way to determine how they would like to receive love. Notice what they ask for from you most often - do they ask for a foot or back rub for you to text them during your day? Does your partner react with over-the-top excitement when you give them a gift, or do they gush when you perform a simple act of service? When you find out your partner's love language, you will see that magic that happens when you express your love to them in their love language! To learn more about The 5 Love Languages® and take a quiz to discover your love language, please go to https://www.5lovelanguages.com/.

ASSIGNMENT 4

Talk with your partner about each of your love languages. Ask them what you can do to help them feel loved. Are your love languages similar or different? How can you work together to help both of you feel loved?

What to Expect - Managing Your Expectations

What to expect as a stepparent can be summed up in three words: Expect The Unexpected.

The stories you may hear in stepparent support groups are staggering. Judges, commissioners, mediators, ex-spouses, partners of ex-spouses, and our partners can sometimes show horrible judgment. There is legal inequality, a lack of resources for divorcing parents, mental illness, controlling ex-spouse; the list is long and bleak. I've heard stories of judges choosing to keep the child with the abusive or neglectful parent; a legal battle over embryo storage from the first marriage/relationship; one parent refusing to drop off a child even one minute early to the other parent's house; parents denying opportunities to children in sports, travel (family or school-related), weddings, funerals, and on and on. One of my stepmom friends said she tries to think of the logical thing to do, then assumes the biological mother of her stepchildren will do the complete opposite because that's been her experience with her co-parent.

Not all situations are extreme, but all situations are unpredictable. (As I was writing this chapter, my stepdaughter came into the room, laid on the floor, and asked me what I was doing. When I told her what this section was about, she immediately started doing a combination of yoga and gymnastics and said, "I bet you didn't expect this!" I love that girl.) The point is, anytime another person is involved in your life, they're going to surprise you, disappoint you, offend you, or do something entirely different than you expect or want them to do, even if they're doing it unintentionally. And, chances are, just when you start to feel like being a stepparent is comfortable and predictable, something is bound to change.

Don't worry; there are some things you can count on; you can expect to feel angry, frustrated, sad, irritated, taken for granted, lonely, hurt, ignored, or resentful. Conversely, in most step-parenting relationships, you will find you frequently feel happy, peaceful, respected, listened to, helped, and filled with love. There are times when you will come first, and there will be other times when the children will. In a blended family, you all have to adjust to each other. Successfully blending a family requires flexibility with things like traditions, parenting time, travel, work, transportation, holidays, school events, vaccinations, religion and spirituality, haircuts, meals, and the list goes on and on indefinitely.

You can also expect that things will be difficult. In any long-term relationship or marriage, learning how to adjust to different personalities, insecurities, function (or dysfunction), your families of origin, and the issues you have experienced in your lives makes things more challenging. If you know going into your relationship that things will be hard at times, you will be less surprised when they turn out that way, and you will be more grateful when things are more manageable.

Create a Plan

Like most couples, Chris and I have had some ridiculous fights. If we entered our marriage prepared with strategies and skills to resolve conflicts successfully or deal with each other's quirks, we would have avoided many stupid arguments. Now, after more than a decade of marriage, I know not to criticize baseball, Dr. Pepper, or professional wrestling, and he knows that I'm irrational about how much I love my dogs.

Talk with your partner about how to deal with the unexpected. Some possible obstacles you might encounter are listed below. Discuss them with your partner:

- What happens when your partner gets off work late, and the co-parent won't allow the stepparent to pick the children up?
- What happens when you sign the stepchildren up for activities, and your co-parent refuses to allow them to participate?
- What happens when the co-parent signs them up for a sport or class, and it's during your parenting time?
- What happens if you and the co-parent have different opinions on how your stepchildren dress, how they will eat, if you will allow sleepovers, what kind of movies you will feel comfortable watching, video games, etc.

There is an idiom that wisely says, "If you fail to plan, you plan to fail." Even though it is impossible to plan for each and every situation that comes at you, you can put in place a few plans to help successfully navigate the rough road that step-parenting can create.

Plan how you'll handle your feelings without letting them ruin your day.
(Practice your social and emotional skills!)

Plan how you can deal with frustrations when you have your stepchildren with you. (Communicate, communicate, communicate!)

Plans in these circumstances help you be more flexible. The more flexible you can be (within boundaries you feel good about), the easier your relationship with the co-parent and your partner will be.

Lower Your Expectations

I've found that the best way for me to deal with the unexpected in co-parenting is to lower all my expectations to zero. When I expected my stepdaughters' mom would pay 50% of medical bills, get them to us on time for us to take them to doctor appointments, transport them like she said she would, buy medication for the kids, or buy their school supplies, I was disappointed and irritated. I was much less frustrated when I expected she would not be the type of parent I am and would mother in a way that was comfortable for her.

Maya Angelou said, "When people show you who they are, believe them the first time." If I had learned this lesson early in my marriage and not expected my co-parent to parent as I do, it would have saved me so much time and frustration. Now that I have learned not to control people and outcomes and come to each situation from neutral, I am much calmer. I'm not giving my girls' mom a pass, and I am human, so I still get irritated from time to time, but I've learned that I'd rather do what I believe to be in the best interest of my stepdaughters instead of trying to be right or the "better parent."

ASSIGNMENT 5

Think about what your expectations are, and prioritize the ones that are most important to you. Talk to your partner about these and see if you both feel the same way. Write notes in the box below.

ASSIGNMENT 6

If your expectations aren't the same, what is different? Are you willing to compromise with your partner or vice versa? What will you do when your expectations are not met?. Write in the box below.

ASSIGNMENT 7

Think about the areas in which you're most willing to be flexible. Discuss these with your partner. Use the box below to take notes.

ASSIGNMENT 8

Write down your thoughts about each of your expectations, now that you have discussed them with your partner. Do you agree with their perspective? Do you want to try to change some of them? Were there any things on your list that were non-negotiable? .

The Best Advice - Let Go Of Expectations

One day I was venting to my mom (which I frequently did) when she gave me some of the best advice I've ever received about stepparenting. I can't specifically remember what my co-parent did that frustrated me that day, but I remember being angry because I am infertile and can't have children of my own, and I was sure that I would be a better parent than many biological moms. My mom asked me, "What if you just treat them like they are your kids? What if, instead of expecting (my co-parent) to pay her share or drive the kids anywhere, you just act like they are solely your responsibility anyway and do everything?" Wow!

Of course, this advice didn't permit me to overstep my role. But it did help me see that I needed to stop expecting my co-parent to take care of the girls like I wanted her to. I was so caught up in how I thought things needed to be, actions that I felt were unfair, and my expectations for how my co-parent should take care of my stepdaughters that I lost sight of the most important thing – my stepdaughters' needs.

After this big "Ah-Ha" moment, the way I behaved as a stepmother and co-parent shifted. It no longer mattered to me which of my stepdaughters' parents was taking them to appointments, school, and important events, or who paid or put effort into meeting their needs. What changed? My paradigm. My stepdaughters and their well-being became the number one priority, not which of their parents was doing things the "right way."

Disengaging from what my co-parent does or does not do has helped me tremendously. I no longer blamed, judged, or became angry at her for not fulfilling her role as my stepdaughter's biological mom in the way I thought she should have. I began to make appointments during our parenting time and arrange for transportation. Instead of expecting her to pay for half of the medical costs and extracurricular activities, we just took the responsibility to pay for them ourselves. It's wasn't fair or right, but that isn't what mattered. When we stepparents give our stepchildren what they need instead of what we think is fair, we disengage from power struggles with the co-parent and keep our sanity.

Letting go of your expectations for the co-parent isn't a foolproof method of creating harmony in your blended family, and it isn't easy, especially if you are a perfectionist or recovering control freak like me. It can feel really one-sided and incredibly frustrating; however, letting go of your expectations as situations arise is a great opportunity to practice your social/emotional skills. The following assignments will help you think about how your life could change if you drop your expectations of your co-parent and focus only on what you can control.

ASSIGNMENT 9

Think about your co-parenting relationship; what are some of the things you are currently trying to control that you need to release? Use the box below.

ASSIGNMENT 10

What would change if you gave up trying to make sure everything in your co-parenting was fair? Write your answer in the box below.

ASSIGNMENT 11

What small changes can you make, right now, in your attitude or behavior with your co-parent that will make your life easier? Answer in the box below.

What is Your Role?

Misunderstanding your role as a stepparent is a preventable but common mistake. How you show up as a stepparent is unique to your own blended family's situation. Ultimately, the decision about what role you will play as a stepparent is up to you, your partner, and to some degree, your stepchildren. It is essential for you to include your stepchildren in the conversation about your roles so they feel heard, validated, and important, especially in this area that has a significant impact on their lives. This discussion may be uncomfortable, but it is vital because it can negatively impact the whole family if you are unclear on your role or step out of the role others expect you to play.

Every custody situation is different, so each stepparent will uniquely fit into their blended family. Sometimes, children have two functioning, caring parents who are excellent at filling each child's individual needs for guidance and authority. In this case, the stepchildren would not need you to step in and function as a parent but might love it if you were a trusted friend and ally.

In other families, one of the biological parents may not be a healthy role model, so their interaction with their children might be limited due to lack of desire or court order. In some families, the biological parent may be completely absent. Perhaps, your co-parent has shared custody but is still not functioning well in general and cannot take care of their children's needs. In this case, you may need to step up as a stepparent and take on a role that requires more responsibility, authority, guidance, and involvement.

In my family, I viewed myself as the most responsible and knowledgeable mother for my stepdaughters in terms of education and medical care, but I also felt like my hands were somewhat tied. My husband was worried about doing something that would cause him to have less time with his daughters, and I didn't want to overstep my boundaries. I very much saw my role as a second mother to my girls, even though they have never called me mom. As with all families, we have had some growing pains, but my stepdaughters are REALLY great, and they're a huge part of why my stepparenting experience has overall been a positive one.

Your role as a stepparent is going to be different than mine. If you have full custody of your stepchildren, you'll be a full-time mother or father. If your stepchildren are young, you may need to take a more active role in raising them, even if your custody is only part-time. You can also expect that your role as a stepparent will change over time, especially if you come into your role as a stepparent while the children are young. If you have adult stepchildren, you'll have to figure out if/what they want in your relationship. Maybe you will all feel more comfortable as an aunt-type figure to your stepchildren if they are already grown.

Don't Forget Your Other Roles
Being defined solely by one role in our lives is unhealthy. Narrowly focusing on our role as a stepparent, and excluding all our other interests, leads us to feel unappreciated, taken advantage of, depressed, and unfulfilled. Don't forget that being a stepparent is essential, but it isn't your only role. You're also a partner, a friend, a daughter or son, a brother or sister, a niece or nephew, an entrepreneur,

an employee, a traveler, someone who loves food, knitting, or exercise, and so much more. It's easy to get wrapped up in the role of stepparenting and forget all the other fantastic things that you love and that help to define you. Don't fall into that trap; you have outstanding, unique qualities. Also, remember that it's never too late to redefine who you are in your relationships. We can always grow, change, and become better. We can continually develop new interests and hobbies and use those activities to make new friendships when feeling lonely.

ASSIGNMENT 12

Discuss with your partner how they perceive your role. Do you have similar expectations? If not, what would you like to change? Use the box below.

ASSIGNMENT 13

If your stepchildren are old enough, discuss with them what they, and you, want your role to be. Do you agree or disagree with them? Is there a way to compromise so you're all happier? Write down your ideas here.

ASSIGNMENT 14

What other roles do you play besides stepparent? What roles are vital for you to keep as you are involved in the lives of your partner's children? Use the box below.

ASSIGNMENT 15

As you consider your role as a stepparent, decide whether you've gotten too caught up in this one role. If so, what would help you step back a little? How can you move towards your other roles?

How to Communicate With Your Co-Parent

Poor communication is one of the primary sources of frustration among blended families and can lead to many challenges for you, your partner, and your co-parent. It is important to note that not all co-parented or blended families come from a partner's divorce or the death of a parent. Sometimes you are parenting a child born due to a short-term relationship or a fling. Sometimes your partner has had multiple relationships and children with multiple partners. No matter how your blended family came to be, communication is one of the most common areas of conflict for blended families, and your partner's relationship history will influence how well you communicate with your co-parent.

Before you came onto the scene, your partner and their ex had a way they communicated. Their communication style is a pattern they developed over time, and in some manner, it may be somehow working for them. Even if all they do is argue over text, they're still engaging in an established pattern of communication that, chances are, they're not open to changing.

Sometimes stepparents try to become involved in the communication patterns, believing it's easier for the stepparent to communicate with the co-parent because they don't have a strained relationship history with the ex. While it may be true that you, as the stepparent, may be a more neutral party, many biological parents tend to resent your intrusion and don't want to communicate with you. In most cases, the co-parent has no legal obligation to talk to you and may strongly prefer to communicate in the established pattern of talk/text/email/message only with your partner.

I have seen stepparents label co-parents as "high-conflict" because they do not wish to communicate about their children with anyone other than their child's other parent. A co-parent is not being high-conflict for refusing to talk to you, they may be high-conflict for different reasons, but this is not one of them. Imagine that you and your partner have children together, then separate. Would you want to communicate with the new person in your former partner's life? Does it seem likely that you might resent that intrusion into your life and want to talk only to your child's other parent? Many biological parents feel this way, and it's not your right to force them to speak to you. If my husband's ex-wife doesn't want to talk to me about things related to my stepchildren, she doesn't have to. I may not like it, but that's her right.

In my coaching practice, I have seen many situations when a stepparent and their partner communicate with the biological parent together, out of necessity. In this arrangement, the ex-partners are usually high-conflict, personal attacks are happening, and there may be a history of domestic abuse. All of these are highly emotional scenarios that require careful communication. Sometimes, one parent asks their partner to help them communicate with their ex to make sure what they're saying is not inflammatory, misread, or misinterpreted before sending a message. In some families, the court will order all communication through an app. In all of these scenarios, apps such as Talking Parents™ (https://talkingparents.com) or Our Family Wizard® (https://ourfamilywizard.com) are beneficial. A family communication app will keep track of all messages and is admissible in court or mediation to implement support for the parents and track how children are doing.

The way we communicate in words, ideas, tone, and gestures does not always accurately convey to the listener our meaning: our upbringing, native language, and background all influence how we communicate and how we understand what other people are saying. You can unintentionally multiply communication errors if you bring another person into a conversation. In any relationship, communication can be challenging. You may think you are communicating with your co-parent clearly and unemotionally. Still, they may become offended or completely misunderstand your intentions or words, which can lead to hurt feelings, frustration, and animosity between you, your co-parent, and your partner.

Think before you speak. This simple phrase is helpful when communicating with your partner and anyone involved in parenting decisions for your blended family. Intentionally decide, with your partner, who is the best person to communicate with your co-parent. In the end, you may decide that the best person to communicate with them is you, but be aware that this decision may also cause the co-parent to react in unforeseen ways.

If you are struggling to communicate effectively with your co-parent or partner, seek guidance from a therapist. They can help you learn how to better express your ideas and emotions to allow deeper connections and more healthy relationships.

ASSIGNMENT 16

Who communicates with your co-parent? Is this working for you? Write down ways this may or may not be working.

ASSIGNMENT 17

Talk to your partner about your current communication styles. Discuss what is working for you and identify areas where you need to improve..

ASSIGNMENT 18

Think about your communication with your co-parent. Can it be improved? Discuss your thoughts with your partner and decide, together, how or if you need to change.

ASSIGNMENT 19

If you are currently communicating with your co-parent, do you want to continue? If not, make a plan to transition the communication to your partner. Make notes below.

The "F" Word - Finances

Finances are a tricky topic for most of us. When we think or talk about money, we tend to get emotional: excited when we get money we weren't expecting, stressed when we have an expense that was not in our budget, worried about meeting our financial obligations, angry when expenses arise that take money from something we were saving for, overwhelmed when we think about the rising costs of basic needs, etc. Money can be a complex subject in any family, especially a blended family, and no single solution works best for everyone. Fortunately, there are options to discuss as you determine how to make finances work in your family.

Various Ways to Manage Income and Bills

Combining–This option works best for families who have no debt and where both partners make approximately equal money. (Debt includes back payments on child support where the government can garnish paychecks.)

Splitting By Percentage–In this option, partners determine how much they each make, totaling 100%. For example, one partner brings in 70% of the combined income; the other makes 30%, they then split the bills and expenses by the percentage 70/30.

Dividing Equally–This option works well for people who make a similar income, so each partner is responsible for 50% of the household bills and expenses.

Using Separate Bank Accounts–Some partners like to have separate accounts, which gives each partner freedom to spend their money how they want or need to and allows for more flexibility. In this scenario, there would be one shared account for bills and household expenses, and each partner would have a separate account for discretionary spending.

However you choose to handle your income and pay your bills, blended families will greatly benefit from hiring a financial planner or using other financial planning resources to help you make decisions regarding budget, saving, investing, and inheritance. A third, neutral party to advise you about spending and saving your money can help alleviate some of the tension created between partners when discussing finances.

Financial Complications

Finances can be further complicated in blended families where both partners have children from previous relationships. Depending on the custody arrangements, one partner's children may live with either parent for significantly more time than the other parent. Usually, this means that spending is disproportionately divided between your partner and their ex, and sometimes between your children and their children, leading to one parent who feels like their children are not treated equally. Unfortunately, the expenses cannot be equally divided in this situation, and sometimes the children from one partner will have more opportunities than their stepsiblings.

As adults, it is our responsibility to look for any inequalities within our blended families and rectify the situations as much as possible. Sometimes, there may be things we can do to help create balance for our children, provide better opportunities for activities, and make sure their wants and needs are met; sometimes, we cannot make the changes we would like. When we can't make changes to create more equality due to financial obstacles, we can expect feelings of hurt, injustice, frustration, remorse, or guilt, etc.

All parents want what is best for their children. We all try to avoid hurt feelings where possible. But even in first marriages, every child has a different experience as they grow up; it is just part of the natural progression of life. In blended families, this is also true. Sometimes children miss out on opportunities they want because their biological parents are separated or because of a disparity in each of their parents' incomes. It is not fair to the children, and it hurts us as parents to see our children in pain, but it is just a fact of life.

We cannot fix the pain our children will experience due to their parents' separation and different living conditions. We cannot keep them from feeling disappointed when finances stand in the way of their hopes and dreams. However, we can help them learn how to deal with life's challenges that in a way that helps them learn from them. We first have to learn to manage our own emotions around money and financial equity to do this.

Finally, as partners and co-parents, we must communicate effectively about finances and decisions such as what "wants" are we ok with saying no to, what needs/wants are important to us that they receive, and what wants/needs/or experiences are imperative to us that our children have.

ASSIGNMENT 20

Which option for managing finances do you think works best for your family? What do you like about that option?

Which option for managing finances does your *partner* think will work best for your family? What do *they* like about that option?

ASSIGNMENT 21

As you discuss the different options for managing finances, which one do you agree is the best fit for your family? Why do you feel like that one will work best? Decide on this together, then put a plan in place to implement any needed changes. Use the box below.

ASSIGNMENT 22

Talk with your children or stepchildren to develop a list of their wants/needs/activities that you need to work into your budget. Discuss this list with your partner and create a plan for discussing it with your co-parent. Create opportunities for a win/win situation that will meet everyone's needs involved.

CHAPTER 5

Building Relationships

Get Intentional About Your Relationships

In Chapters Two and Three, we talked about your most important relationship - your relationship with yourself and the person you want to be, your highest self. Then we discussed your identity as a co-parent and your life in a blended family. All of your work so far has been in preparation to tackle the last two most challenging chapters in this workbook. In particular, this chapter discusses external relationships and how to improve them. Then, in the final chapter in this workbook, you will develop a plan of how to handle conflict when it inevitably arises, which it absolutely will.

In case you can't tell yet, I'm a huge fan of living mindfully and intentionally, which can make a huge difference when it comes to step-parenting. One of the benefits of shared custody is that unlike single parents or nuclear families, you have some time off from parenting and don't have to deal with your stepchildren or co-parent in your home 24/7. Having scheduled time away from your stepchildren and co-parent allows you the distance you need to decide how you want to approach current challenges and determine what you want from your relationships. We cannot entirely control our relationships, but when we take time to step back and reflect on what is going on and decide what actions we will take, it helps us build the kind of life and relationships we want.

First, let's take a quick look at the four most important external relationships in your life: Your relationship with your partner, your relationship with your stepchildren, your relationship with the co-parent, and your relationship with your in-laws.

1-Your Relationship With Your Partner

Your most important external relationship is with your partner. When you think about your relationship with your partner, think about how you want it to function. Some of these questions can help guide you through creating a picture of how you want your relationship with your partner to be. (Refer to this list of questions for Assignment 1 in this chapter.)

- What kind of relationship do you want with them? Are you equal partners in your romance, parenting roles, and life?
- Are you sexually compatible with your partner? Do you discuss your sexual relationship openly and

intimately? Are you mutually fulfilled?
- Do you communicate well, often, and truthfully?
- What qualities are essentia, to you,l in a relationship? To your partner?
- Is your partner your best friend?
- Do you share common interests and pay attention to your partner's interests, even if they do not appeal to you?
- Do you look out for each other's best interests?
- Are you selfless in your partnership?
- Do you fight regularly? If so, do you resolve conflict in a healthy way?
- Do you talk about complicated subjects openly?

It is important to remember that no marriage or partnership is perfect. But don't allow yourself to lose hope when you think about what your relationship is and what it is not. Instead, realize that we all have areas in our partnerships that we need to work on, and this is a good thing. It allows you to grow and become better. Remember that to progress in life, we need to become uncomfortable, and it can be very distressing when we take a step back and take inventory of our relationships. However, this is actually a good thing because it reminds us of who we want to become and can help us come together to overcome weaknesses in our relationships and set goals towards something better.

However, sometimes when we take inventory of our relationships, we face some really complicated truths. We all want to believe that our chosen partners are the people we need them to be, but that may not be the case for you. If that's true in your situation, you have some hard decisions to make about your future. I highly recommend seeking advice from a therapist to help you decide how you want to move forward in your life.

2-Your Relationship With Your Stepchildren

Your second most important external relationship is the one you will build with your stepchildren. Even though you may have children of your own, we will only deal with your relationship with your stepchildren here. The relationship with each child is unique and changeable. As frustrating as it may be, the relationship you have with each of your stepchildren is always going to be somewhat out of your control. While you have absolute authority over your thoughts, beliefs, and actions regarding your stepchildren, other people also affect this relationship, mainly your co-parent and the stepchildren themselves. They may welcome you as a stepparent, friend, or another person to love and care for them. Or, they may see you as a threat, an obstacle to their hopes for their parents to get back together, or they may resent you for taking their biological parent's place in your partner's life. Your stepchild may also view you as unimportant and keep you at arm's length with no desire for a relationship with you at all.

My relationship with my stepdaughters has changed over time. When I first met my husband, the girls were two and four and needed help with almost everything. They have since transitioned into adults have jobs and want significantly less of my help in their lives. My 20-year-old stepdaughter has graduated from high school and is a pretty typical young adult. She wants to control her life and decisions and doesn't want interference from anyone, especially her parents. Her progression from a child to a teen to a high school graduate has changed our relationship multiple times. My 18-year-old stepdaughter still accepts help from me from time to time, but for the most part, she is responsible for her decisions and how she spends her time. Transitioning our relationship has been rough at times and requires significant flexibility from all of us. It helps to think of relationships with stepchildren as a dance. Sometimes I lead, sometimes my husband leads, sometimes my daughter leads, and sometimes, unfortunately, my co-parent tries to cut in. In the end, what matters most, is that we are all on the dance floor, trying not to step on each other's toes.

Some questions to consider when you are thinking about your relationship with your stepchild and how you can improve it are:
- Have I asked my stepchild what they want from me? Am I willing to listen to their answer and be that person?
- Am I willing to fulfill the role my stepchild needs?
- Have I made an effort to get to know my stepchild?
- What kind of participation does my partner need from me?
- How do I know when things are going well? How do I know when things are going poorly?
- Am I open to receiving feedback from my stepchild without taking it personally?
- Am I careful to keep my frustration/anger/resentment about the co-parent from my relationship with my stepchild?

3-Your Relationship With Your Co-parent

The third most important external relationship is with your stepchild's other parent, your co-parent. Unfortunately, you have even less influence in this relationship than you do with your stepchildren because this relationship will undoubtedly come with a lot of baggage. In the perfect situation, you may have a fantastic relationship with the co-parent: you might be friends, and they may view you as the asset you are, someone they can count on to help out with their children and who can love and protect them as if they were your own. Then, there is the other side of the coin, and depending on your co-parent, you may not be able to have a positive influence on your relationship with them at all. They may blame you, criticize you, ignore you, or despise you no matter how hard you try or how much you want to have a good relationship with them. When your co-parent is determined to dislike you, your choices are limited to how you react, communicate, and interact. This relationship, like all relationships, will change over time and has the potential to improve. Sadly, in cases where there is unaddressed trauma, significant mental illness, addiction, or personality disorder, it may not change for the better.

4-Your Relationship With Your In-laws

The fourth external relationship you will want to spend some time contemplating is the one you have with your in-laws. I am fortunate to have in-laws that support my husband, and by extension, me, but that's not always the case. Some stepparents I have worked with have in-laws who have chosen the ex's side, even over their own child. When your in-laws choose your co-parent over you, it creates a complicated dynamic, especially because it makes it feel like they may be working against you and your partner. Remember, your in-laws' relationship with your co-parent is a necessary part of your stepchildren's lives because they are their grandparents; it isn't always a reflection of their perception of your worth as a partner or as a stepparent. Yes, it can hurt when your in-laws spend time with your co-parent, buy them gifts, spend holidays with them, or invite them over for special occasions if they are not treating you equally, but remember, this is no reflection on you or your worth as a person, a partner, or a parent. You get to decide what type of relationship you want to have with your in-laws. The proverb "kill them with kindness" goes a long way here. If you want them involved in your stepchildren's lives (and they should be, as long as they are a healthy influence), treat them as if you already have the kind of relationship you want, always giving the benefit of the doubt and the opportunity to show up. Even though they will decide how to treat you, in the long run, what matters is making sure you are doing what is best for you, your partner, and your stepchildren and acting accordingly.

ASSIGNMENT 1

Look at the list of questions in Part 1 to help you determine what kind of relationship you currently have with your partner. Then, decide what you WANT to have. Write a list of ways you can improve to help guide you as you work towards creating the kind of relationship you want.

ASSIGNMENT 2

Discuss the list you created in Assignment 1 with your partner. Is your relationship on the right track? What changes, if any, is your partner willing to make?

ASSIGNMENT 3

Assess your relationship with your stepchildren. How can you improve? Decide on one or two actions that will make the most significant impact on your relationship and commit to them.

ASSIGNMENT 4

What kind of relationship would you like to have with your partner's ex? Are you willing or able to set aside old hurts to move the relationship in a positive direction? Write your answers below.

ASSIGNMENT 5

What relationship do you have with your in-laws? What type of relationship do they want to have with you? (If you don't know, talk to them about this) What are you willing to do to make the positive changes necessary to have the type of relationship that will most positively benefit your stepchildren? Write your answrs below.

Successful Partnerships/Marriages Take Effort

When you decide to pursue a relationship with someone who has children, you choose to give time and space to their children. Let me repeat that: you made this choice to have your stepchildren become a part of your life; the extent to which you are involved as a stepparent will vary, but your stepchildren will remain in your life for as long as the relationship continues. This parenting partnership can create some obstacles, especially when you are first learning how to adjust to your new family.

Married couples without children have the luxury of time alone and space away from other family members to learn how to make their partnership work, without the added stress of young children, teens, or young adults who require a significant amount of attention. As a stepparent, you become a part of a family that already has some sort of an established routine; you do not get the luxury of one-on-one, unencumbered relationship development. Conflicts with your co-parent can also add further complications.

All relationships require effort and time as you adjust to having a new person in your life. How do you find the time to make this effort when children are already part of your partner's life? By making your relationship a priority. Prioritizing your partner doesn't mean removing anyone else from your life so you can focus only on the two of you. It does mean making a concerted effort to spend some time together every day, to strengthen intimacy, connection, communication, and friendship.

Begin At The Beginning

- Think about the things that attracted you to your partner in the first place.
- Was it their sense of humor, creativity, or intellect?
- Did you fall in love with the way they parent their children?
- Were you attracted to their spontaneity?
- Did you fall for them because of the way they treated you?
- Which qualities intrigued you the most? Kindness? Sense of justice? Integrity? Humility?
- What did you instantly love about them? How has that love grown?
- How did you feel physically around them? Did you have intense chemistry, either physically or intellectually?
- Do they serve you in a way that you particularly appreciate?

For me, I loved seeing Chris parent his kids. He was so fun with them and clearly loved them. I've grown to appreciate his ability to focus on the positive things that are happening, his love of seeing his family happy, his desire to learn, and his passion for politics. Focus on the positive attributes that first attracted you to your partner instead of focusing on the little things that annoy you. Although the things you love about your partner will change, it's a good idea to keep a running list of qualities and attributes you love about them and keep adding to it over time. Take a moment right now to look at the list you created in the very first assignment of Chapter One. Is there anything you would like to add to it?

Build Your Relationship Through Shared Experiences

We have raised my two stepdaughters from ages two and four. Believe me, I understand how difficult it can be to prioritize your partner when you have little ones. It feels like you never have enough time, money, or energy to do everything you need to do, let alone do the things you would like to do. As kids grow up, though, things change, and while you may still have a great relationship with your stepchildren, they won't live with you forever. The time you spend building your relationship with your partner while raising your family is essential, especially because when the children are gone, you are left with just the two of you. So many couples, even in first marriages, put all their time and energy into raising their family, and then when the children are gone, they find they no longer have anything in common.

How do you put your relationship with your partner first? Here is a list of some things that Chris and I have done:
- Take short vacations or weekends away by ourselves
- Weekly scheduled date nights

- Cook each other's favorite meals
- Discuss how co-parenting and life situations are affecting us
- Take time to check in with how work, life, and parenting are going,
- Activities that we don't love but that the other person likes (in my case, going to baseball games; in Chris's case, walking my dogs).

These are just examples, but hopefully, they get you thinking about what you can do to prioritize your partner. When we prioritize our partners, we focus on building our relationship rather than anything that can interfere or cause a disconnect. You will find greater happiness, security, friendship, and stability when you consistently prioritize your partnership, spend time together, and make sure that you are meeting your own and your partner's needs.

Shared experiences, especially weekly date nights, help you keep your romance alive, encourage communication, and help you foster greater intimacy. I have provided a list of ideas for date nights in **Appendix B**. Keep in mind, date night does not need to be expensive to be worthwhile; sharing time together is the goal. Take a moment right now to complete the first part of Assignment 6 before you proceed with the rest of the chapter.

ASSIGNMENT 6

What is something you and your partner like to do together? Write it down here, then do it in the next two weeks.

Write down how you felt after you did the activity above. Did it help you strengthen your relationship? Was it weird not to focus on the kids for a little while? Journal your thoughts below.

ASSIGNMENT 7

Evaluate how well you're doing at prioritizing your relationship. Write down your thoughts here, then discuss them with your partner.

ASSIGNMENT 8

What do you think you could do to make your relationship more of a priority? Create a plan and discuss it with your partner. Journal your notes below.

Keep Your Relationship Strong by Setting Healthy Boundaries

Even though there are times when your stepchildren have to come first, you and your partner can create space for your relationship by setting healthy boundaries. We all have different ideas of what healthy boundaries are. Setting healthy boundaries is essential for creating a happy life, a successful relationship, and a functioning blended family. Healthy boundaries also naturally evolve as your life changes, your stepchildren grow, and your various relationships change.

How do you create healthy boundaries? By placing limits on how you allow others to interact with you. We can only set boundaries for ourselves. It is a good idea to have a conversation with your partner to define your mutual boundaries and what you will and will not accept when it comes to relationships (partner, co-parent, stepchildren).

Setting Boundaries

When my stepdaughters were young, they pushed back when we encouraged them to set boundaries because they were worried about being mean. Setting boundaries can be very uncomfortable, especially if you are a people pleaser. Children can feel incredibly uneasy about setting firm limits, and adults can unknowingly contribute to this type of hesitancy because they may not understand healthy boundaries. The following table contains some common truths and lies about setting personal boundaries.

Lies About Boundaries	Truths About Healthy Boundaries
Setting boundaires is a way to control others' behaviors.	Setting healthy boundaries is a way to help define what you are or are not willing to accept in the way others behave towards you.
Setting boundaries is unkind.	Clarity is kindness. When you are clear with others about your boundaries, you take ownership of your wellbeing.
Setting boundaries is selfish; it means you think your needs are more important than others' needs.	My needs are valid; your needs are valid. We can interact in a way that allows both of our needs to be met without making either one of us feel uncomfortable, unheard, or invalidated. Flexibility is important, but only to a certain extent; setting healthy boundaries helps us understand to what extent we are willing to be flexible.
Setting boundaries is unrealistic.	It is important to be realistic when you set your boundaries. Only you know what you can and cannot tolerate. It is also just as important to be willing to walk away and be firm when others try to push your boundaries.
Setting boundaries is disrespectful.	I can be both firm and kind when enforcing my boundaries. I understand that when I respect my own boundaries, others will also learn to respect them.

My favorite way to illustrate the importance of boundaries is to explain how I help protect my dogs. I love my dogs! They are my babies, and I would do anything for them! I have a fenced yard that keeps them safe from cars, other dogs, or strangers. Am I selfish, unkind, or controlling to have this boundary for my dogs' protection? Of course not! Is it selfish to keep strangers out of my yard to protect both my dogs and the strangers? No. My fence is a literal boundary, but it also serves as a metaphor for an easy way to demonstrate to children how the boundaries we set as stepparents are there to keep everyone safe.

Healthy boundaries are helpful, especially if you've never set them before or you're not sure how to set them. Healthy boundaries limit physical, mental, emotional, financial, or spiritual interactions with other people. Sometimes, courts determine boundaries for co-parents, like designating a set location for pickup and drop-off.

Examples of what you should discuss with your partner when you are setting healthy boundaries include:
- How will you handle the situation when you are sitting on the sofa enjoying a movie, and a stepchild comes in and wants to sit between you?
- Will you allow your stepchild to co-sleep in bed with you when they are upset at night or have had a nightmare?
- How will you handle calls or texts during a date night?
- How will you manage interruptions when you are having a serious discussion with your partner?
- How will you manage boundary breaches by the co-parent when they try to interfere in your relationship with your partner?
- How strict are you going to be (as a team) when it comes to enforcing the parameters of the custody arrangements? How will you handle it not if, but when your co-parent tries to change your standard custody arrangements?
- How do you want to interact (or not) with your co-parent? (frequency, method, are any subjects off the table for discussion?)
- How much of your time and energy are you willing to give your co-parent or stepchildren? How will you handle a breach of this boundary?
- What are you willing or unwilling to do for your partner? How can you communicate with them to let them know they've asked you to do something you do not want to do or are uncomfortable doing?

Your blended family cannot be strong unless your relationship is strong, and to keep your relationship strong, you must have healthy boundaries. Your stepchildren will learn to respect your role as a stepparent, and they will benefit from watching you and your example as you learn how to have happy and successful relationships by prioritizing your relationship and setting healthy boundaries.

Communicate Your Boundaries

You must communicate your boundaries effectively, especially with your partner, your stepchildren, and your co-parent. Keep in mind, it may not be possible to communicate your boundaries with your co-parent because they don't care or will intentionally try to manipulate you by crossing your boundaries. In any case, have a plan to help you address when others try to push past your boundaries; this is a healthy way to manage relationships and prioritize your well-being. Remember, be clear; clarity is kindness.

Set Boundaries With Your Co-parent

Boundaries are an essential element of a functional relationship with your co-parent. Some co-parents can be demanding, careless, or malicious, and feel entitled to your time and energy; boundaries help protect your well-being. Even if your co-parent is mentally healthy and friendly, you still need boundaries for the relationship to remain functional. Sometimes you may be unable to communicate your boundaries with your co-parent adequately. In that case, just set healthy boundaries and decide what you want to do when they are crossed.

Not all relationships with the co-parent are contentious, but they often are. I'll give some examples of what it looks like when a co-parent, partner, or stepchild breaches boundaries to help drive this point home.

- The co-parent insists/demands that the stepparent babysit the children for an entire summer, regardless of shared custody arrangements.
- Without warning or permission, the co-parent drops off the children at the other parent's house early in the morning or late at night.
- Stepchildren come into the bedroom without knocking.
- Children play with or look at the pictures on their stepparent's phone without permission.
- Mutually agreed upon rules are not being enforced equally in both households.
- Despite child support or alimony payments, co-parents ask for more money to buy extra clothing or additional activities.

As you can see, setting healthy boundaries is extremely important as a stepparent, and it's one of the top things you and your partner should discuss as soon as possible. Of course, if your co-parent is hostile, you'll want to set firm boundaries about the kind of behavior that you're willing to accept from them and stick to it! Also, keep in mind, there will be times when someone will cross a boundary you didn't even know you had or needed. When this happens, make sure you articulate the boundary as soon as possible with both your partner and your co-parent to set the expectation for the next time you interact.

Set Boundaries with the Children

Children are experts at pushing boundaries; it's normal for them to test and try to see what you will allow! Teenagers often think they know better than you and will tell you so. Children don't hesitate at all to interrupt a conversation between adults, walk into a bedroom unannounced, rummage through adults' things, play with an adult's electronics, etc. The best way to help children learn the importance of respecting boundaries is to model the behavior and let them know your expectations, then enforce the limits you have in place. Have regular conversations with your stepchildren to remind them how to respect boundaries; rearticulate your boundaries during these conversations to help your stepchildren understand and discover their boundaries so they can set them with you, your partner, their siblings, and friends.

Without healthy boundaries, you're more likely to feel unsupported, overwhelmed, unappreciated, and unsure. Healthy boundaries help you feel protected, happy, loved, supported, appreciated, and energized. You can, and should, set boundaries with everyone in your life, including your children, partner, and stepchildren. It is important to remember that no two people have the same set of boundaries; your boundaries will look different than your partner's and other stepparents'. Boundaries are about protecting you and your energy, which is why it's so essential that you decide what you want them to be.

How To Articulate Boundaries

Setting and communicating boundaries can be a new concept. It is helpful to demonstrate ways to help others understand your boundaries. Here are a few examples:

- **Use "I" statements** – "I understand your (biological parent) doesn't require you to check-in when you are out late; however, I worry about your safety and feel less anxious when we check in with each other regularly."
- **Use the Good-Boundary-Good method** – "I am so happy you love to cuddle with your dad and me! I love cuddling with your dad, too, and appreciate the time I have with him. Will you come to sit beside him, rather than between us, so we can all feel loved?"
- **Explain the boundary clearly** – "I understand that you would like to pick the children up early Sunday morning; however, the court order specifies that pick-up and drop-off are at noon; we will see you then."
- **Clearly outline the consequences for pushing/breaching the boundary** – "I understand that there are times you feel it is urgent to speak to (your partner) about the children; however, Friday night is our date night, and you repeatedly call us when we are out together. I have requested you not to call us on Friday night. We will be turning our phone ringers off when we are on a date. Please, contact us only by text and only if it is a true emergency. Otherwise, please wait till Saturday to discuss issues that concern the children."
- **Follow through when your boundaries are violated** – "We have established that your phone curfew is 9 p.m. when you are in our home. You did not turn your phone off at 9 p.m. last night, so you will not have your phone for the next 24 hours (or whatever consequence you have already established)."

ASSIGNMENT 7

What boundaries do you want to set for yourself with your partner? Write in the boxes below.

ASSIGNMENT 8

What boundaries do you want to set for yourself with your stepchildren?

ASSIGNMENT 9

What boundaries do you want to set for yourself with your co-parent?

ASSIGNMENT 10

Discuss how you will create healthy boundaries and use the box below to develop a plan of how to address the situation when your partner, stepchildren, or co-parent try to push your boundaries. Use the questions listed above as a guideline.

Healthy Boundaries

When you set healthy boundaries and understand the need for them, especially in a co-parenting relationship, you can more easily understand and respect boundaries set by others. The keyword here is healthy boundaries. Healthy boundaries protect you and your energy and don't try to control others. Boundaries are give and take; when you set your boundaries, you also understand that partners, co-parents, in-laws, children, or stepchildren also have the right to healthy boundaries.

Healthy boundaries come from a place of emotional maturity and are ideally created during an open discussion as biological parents mutually agree upon what they feel is best for their children. For example, a healthy boundary for a stepparent would include a clear understanding of your role and not overstepping your co-parent's role. Another example of a healthy boundary is setting the expectation that all communication is respectful between co-parents, even, and especially if, they are difficult to get along with.

It's best to have a conversation about boundaries before getting into any relationship, but this isn't always possible. My stepdaughters were two and four when I met them and young children don't generally understand what boundaries are or feel comfortable saying "no" to adults. Over time, my stepdaughters have learned to set boundaries with us, such as asking us to knock before coming into their rooms or making sure their voices are heard when choices directly impact them.

The following lists provide examples of healthy boundaries you might want to consider. These lists can give you ideas of where to begin setting boundaries if you, like most adults, are new to the concept of actively setting boundaries.

**Note: Setting boundaries together isn't possible in every co-parenting situation. If it's not possible for you, set healthy boundaries for the children in your own home.

Healthy Boundaries for Parenting in Both Households

- Bedtimes - Discuss and agree to a mutually enforced bedtime; decide how you will enforce the set bedtime.
- Medical decisions - (If your custody agreement does not have details about medical decisions for your stepchildren.) Who is responsible for choosing doctors, scheduling well-checks, etc.? If you want to give vitamin supplements, what type? Who will be in charge of making sure vaccinations are up to date? Who will schedule dental appointments, etc.?
- Education - Which school will your stepchildren attend? How will you enforce homework requirements? Which parent will address teacher feedback? Who will pick up the child when they are sick? How will you communicate to all parents about awards or performances, etc.?
- Entertainment - Which activities will your child attend, view, participate in, etc.? For example, if your stepchild is heading to a sleepover and you know they will be watching a movie, it's helpful to decide in advance which movies are considered age-appropriate and which are not.
- Dietary needs - mutually deciding on how to meet the nutritional needs of the children.

Healthy Boundaries for Your Partner

- Agree to communicate before making decisions for the children to maintain set boundaries for sleepovers, movie nights, friends in bedrooms, internet usage, playdates, etc.
- Agree that all changes in scheduling or custody, vacations, etc., are discussed and acceptable before you make any financial deposits or changes.

Healthy Boundaries for Stepchildren

- **Physical Affection** – Help your stepchild decide what they are okay with when it comes to hugging, cuddling, kisses from other adults, etc. For example, make sure they understand they have the right to say no when an adult wants a hug/kiss from them.
- **Privacy** – They have a right to reasonable privacy in their bedrooms, electronics, journals, phone calls, etc. Have a conversation where they can express their desire for privacy to you; then, the parents will decide how much privacy is age and situation appropriate. For example: establish a

ground rule that the passcodes for electronic devices will always be set by one of the biological parents. Set the expectation that one of the parents will perform random cell phone checks to ensure their safety and that smart online rules are being followed.
- **Sensitive discussions** – Talk with your stepchildren about whether or not they want to discuss things like dating, sex, puberty, etc., with you.

Some boundaries listed above may not be possible for your family. For example, you might have to limit the amount of privacy each child has in their bedrooms or on their electronic devices if they are using drugs, struggling with mental health, engaging in risky sexual behavior, or if you suspect they are bullying or are being bullied by other children.

Unhealthy Boundaries

Most parents are highly protective of their children, which is an innate, survival-driven trait that has evolved in humanity for tens of thousands of years. Sometimes, this instinct to protect our offspring causes parents to create unhealthy boundaries. Motivated by insecurity, jealousy, distrust, over-protectiveness, or need for control, your co-parent may seek to restrict the relationship between you and your stepchildren. Unfortunately, this is a common challenge that stepparents face. An example of this type of unhealthy boundary is when your co-parent tries to set rules for how you interact with their child when they are in your home, or when they place unreasonable limitations on what you, as the stepparent, can or cannot do with "their children." Unhealthy boundaries that prevent you from fully engaging as a stepparent also limit your ability to form a healthy relationship with your stepchildren, which creates a very frustrating situation for all involved.

Even though, in general, we do not need to accept unhealthy boundaries, this particular situation is one that you cannot challenge. Stepparents don't have the same bond with their stepchildren as biological parents. Suppose your co-parent is attempting to control your relationship with their children. In that case, resisting could create a loyalty bind and aggravate an already volatile situation, which may cause your stepchildren to fight against, disregard, or withdraw from you completely. If this happens in your family, the appropriate response is for your partner to speak directly with their ex to resolve the situation, if possible.

Honoring boundaries is a critical part of building trust in all our relationships. When others respect our boundaries, we appreciate and respect theirs in return and vice versa. Your assignments for this section will focus on discussing and implementing boundaries in your core relationships.

ASSIGNMENT 11

Discuss healthy boundaries with your partner. What boundaries are important to them? Do you feel ok with their boundaries? If not, why? Why is it important for you to respect your partner's boundaries, even if you don't agree with them? Journal your thoughts below.

ASSIGNMENT 12

With your partner, discuss boundaries with your stepchildren. What do they understand about boundaries? What boundaries do they want to set for themselves? Encourage them to write their thoughts down. After your discussion, journal your thoughts.

ASSIGNMENT 13

Are there boundaries anyone has set that are difficult for you? Why are they difficult? Journal your thoughts below.

Teamwork

When you join a family with existing rules, discipline styles, and communication patterns, the adjustment period can be tricky, especially when your parenting style differs from your partner or co-parent. Ideally, all parents involved in raising a child will be on the same page for rules, consequences, etc., but this doesn't often happen in co-parenting. Your co-parent may have a different parenting style or do things you dislike. When your stepchild is at their other home, anything that happens there is out of your control. The good news is that you can control your behavior, what happens when your stepchildren are with you, and how you and your partner support each other.

Parents and stepparents who unite in their parenting efforts provide structure and create a family where children feel safe and thrive. If you want your stepchildren to respect you and your home's rules, they need to see a united effort between you and your partner. Often, when our partners feel guilty (about the divorce, custody arrangements, or a lack of consistent parenting by their ex, etc.), they worry that they are being too harsh when they enforce rules and consequences for their children. This is a thinking error; children thrive in structured environments that provide consistency, predictability, and routines. The more you and your partner provide stability in your home, the better off the children will be.

In situations of parental alienation, you may have to be flexible because your co-parent is attempting to create a wedge between your partner and their children, which means that any attempts to set rules and expectations in your home may result in unfounded allegations of abuse. (More about parental alienation in Chapter Six.)

When you become a stepparent, chances are your stepchildren won't automatically respect you, especially if they're adolescents or adults. Your partner can help your stepchildren learn to respect you by emphasizing your role as an authority figure and communicating that they fully support what you say. Even if everyone involved in raising your stepchildren has different parenting styles, you can learn to agree about what works best for the family, which might mean you need to reevaluate your expectations about bedtimes, phone time, homework, clothing, hair color/style, etc. When you create a team dynamic in your home, you learn how to be flexible and deliberate about which battles you are willing to fight. Remember, as a stepparent, you are coming into an already established family, even if it isn't working in a healthy or positive way. Your role is to be a supportive partner, an authority figure, and an advocate for the stepchildren. You will find success in your role when you choose to all play on the same team.

ASSIGNMENT 14

Identify your priorities and standards for raising your stepchildren.

ASSIGNMENT 15

Talk with your partner about their priorities for raising their children. Are their priorities the same as yours or not?

ASSIGNMENT 16

Talk with your partner about parenting your stepchildren. What is working well? What is not working? Are there areas where change is necessary? Are you open to making an effort to change?

It's Going to Happen — What To Do When Your Partner Prioritizes the Children

Let's face it; there will be times when your partner will choose their children over you and your relationship, especially if you have younger stepchildren who need more parental involvement. Sometimes this is necessary and a good choice, and sometimes it is not necessary and can hurt your relationship.

Many factors affect how we spend our time. Your partner may prioritize time with their children when they feel guilty about how the divorce has affected them or if they're stressed about trying to create a balance between work, children, and your relationship. They may choose to spend time with their children to avoid conflict, especially if you are struggling in your relationship. Your partner's emotional health or family dynamics may also be a factor when they choose to put their children first because they may perceive a threat to their child's wellbeing.

The problem here is not necessarily that your partner is prioritizing their children, which in and of itself is not wrong. The choice to put children and their needs first becomes a problem when you feel like your partner's emphasis on taking care of the children's (perceived) needs in disregard to all else is unwarranted. When your stepchildren aren't in immediate danger, and they don't have unmet needs, or if you're struggling and you need someone to support you, where your partner chooses to focus their time and energy can create a roadblock to a successful relationship.

Your reaction in this situation depends on your perception of your partner's motivations. If you are using thinking errors (and we all use them), your actions will result in negative thoughts and behaviors. If you believe your partner is acting selfishly, you might react in anger or withdraw. If you believe your partner always chooses the kids over you, you may feel bitter and taken for granted. If you think your partner doesn't love you as much as they love their children, you may become lonely and depressed. As you identify and correct your thinking errors, you will become skilled at reframing how you interpret others' actions. Instead of believing they are trying to avoid spending time with you, you can view how they choose to spend their time as evidence of their commitment to their parental responsibilities and devotion to their children.

To change how you react when your partner chooses the children over you, you'll want to use three key skills: communication, mindset work, and coping skills.

For example, you feel unimportant and left out because your partner spends all their free time with their children.
1. Communicate: Use "I feel" statements to communicate your feelings in a way that does not blame or shame your partner. "I feel" statements will help them understand that you are taking responsibility for your feelings while acknowledging that they are valid and need to be addressed.
2. Mindset Work: Identify your thinking errors about your partner's choices, then reframe how you interpret them. It helps if you ask them to clarify their motivations to understand their thoughts better. Your partner may not even realize that they're prioritizing their children over you, or they may recognize their behavior but aren't sure how to change.
3. Coping skills: Find ways to meet your needs and help you feel fulfilled when your partner spends time with their children. For example, suppose your partner takes your stepchildren to the park for some one-on-one time. Rather than spending that time brooding about how you feel left out, do something nice for yourself: read a book, work out, learn a new skill, or find a hobby. Remember, your happiness in life is entirely up to you.

It can be challenging to change thoughts and feelings about our place in our relationship and our partner's priorities, especially when we have felt neglected in the past. Humans tend to believe our thoughts and feelings are facts; they're not; they're just our thoughts and feelings. It's challenging to remember to rein in our thoughts, especially in the heat of the moment when we experience intense emotions. It takes practice to retrain our brains and build new neural pathways. When negative, blaming, or self-deprecating thoughts creep in, stop and ask yourself, "Is this true?" If the thoughts are true, then make a conscious decision, followed by effort, to change the situation. If your thoughts are not true, look for your thinking error, find evidence that it is untrue, then turn around the statement to be one that is.

Here is an example of how to change your mindset and reframe. You begin by thinking, "My partner always puts the children's needs first. My needs don't matter to them." Ask yourself, "Is this true?" or "Is this always true?" In this case, the answer is almost always that the thinking error is not true. Then, look for evidence that it is NOT TRUE, and reframe your thinking error to "My partner needs to be with their children right now. They show their love and commitment to our family by helping care for the children's needs." For an extra powerful jolt to change that thinking error, add in the self-love statement, "I am a priority to my partner, and I am a priority to myself. I can meet my own needs."

Placing your fulfillment and happiness in the hands of another person is not only risky; it is dangerous to your self-esteem and puts undue pressure on your partner. It is vital to create differentiation in your partnership, which means your identity and self-esteem are not dependent on others, including your romantic relationship, parental partnerships, or your relationships with your stepchildren. When you have differentiation in your life, your self-esteem is entirely self-sufficient and self-sustaining; you do not look outward for inward validation; you understand it is okay to have different needs, opinions, and values than your partner.

When you neglect yourself and do not meet your own needs, and you feel like you are a second or even third priority. Find fulfillment by making sure that you are doing things in your life that make you happy and create joy. If you are happy, you're less likely to be frustrated with your partner and their children's needs.

So what do you do when your partner prioritizes the children's needs? Whatever brings you happiness or joy outside of your family. You can have a night out with friends, read a book, watch a movie, go to the gym, go to the symphony, take a hike, drive down to the river or beach and watch the waves, take a walk, etc. The possibilities are limited only by your imagination. Another benefit to finding fulfillment outside of your family is that you will be a better partner when you return from doing something you love. As you take time to reconnect with your partner and your stepchildren, your bucket of kindness and happiness will be overflowing, and you'll have plenty of love to share because you are meeting your own needs.

ASSIGNMENT 17

Write down your thoughts and beliefs about your partner putting their children first.

ASSIGNMENT 18

How do these thoughts make you feel?

ASSIGNMENT 19

How can you reframe these thoughts into something more helpful?

ASSIGNMENT 20

What do you want to do to help you feel better when your partner puts their children's needs ahead of yours?

ASSIGNMENT 21

What are your "go-to" coping skills? What makes you feel better when you're upset or hurt? If you don't have any, see the list in **Appendix A** and choose several that you can try. As you're thinking through this list, choose some that you can use in any situation (work, home, etc.) Write them down somewhere you'll see them often and practice them daily.

Building A Relationship with Your Stepchildren

Building a relationship with stepchildren is easiest when they're young. Younger children tend to love and accept everyone, like how they make friends at the park or playground just by asking someone to be friends. Children of elementary age and younger are more open to new relationships, especially with people who show genuine interest in them or are kind to them (unless parental alienation is happening, more about this in Chapter Six).

Young Stepchildren

If you're fortunate to have younger stepchildren like I was, there are many things you can do to build a relationship with them. Focus on their interests and hobbies, even if you're not interested in those things. Try new activities with them. Take them out hiking, swimming, or to the park, blow bubbles, run through the sprinklers, or play sidewalk games. When they are with you, enroll them in sports or activities, and then be their biggest cheerleader on the sidelines. Other activities could include paint nights, making crafts, building a fort, cooking fun meals, or sharing with them something you enjoyed as a child. Find a hobby that you can do, just the two of you, to create special bonding moments. The more time you spend with your young stepchildren, the better relationship you'll build with them. I've found this to be so true with both of my stepdaughters. My oldest loves Marvel movies, and when I listen to her talk about them, she will easily talk to me for a while. It's a great way to show her I care about her life and interests, even if I don't care about superheroes.

As children grow up, they tend to become more guarded, defensive, and loyal to their biological parents, which makes it more difficult, as a stepparent, to build a relationship with them. Older children, including adult stepchildren, may have no interest in being close, building a relationship, or even in acknowledging you. Of course, this is difficult. It hurts to be excluded and rejected, especially when the people rejecting you are loved by and close to your partner. Unfortunately, when adolescents and adults are involved, it takes much more effort, patience, and kindness to break past these barriers. It is helpful if you can enlist the support and help of your partner to encourage their children to at least show the minimum of respect and kindness towards you.

Older Stepchildren

What NOT To Do

It can be helpful to see a list of what not to do when you are working on building a relationship with older stepchildren:
- Do not attempt to regulate, interfere, or limit access to their parents, even if you are trying to protect them from a toxic biological parent - this will backfire on you.
- Do not expect an easy friendship or relationship, do not try to force a relationship. Instead, show respect, kindness, and be their advocate when needed.
- Do not attempt to define appropriate boundaries for them. You cannot tell them what to think or how to feel. Respect their boundaries.
- Do not try to fix them.

What TO DO

Now that we know what not to do, let's focus on what we can do:
- Learn how the family communicates and honor it.
- Be kind and respectful, even if they are not reciprocating.
- Invite them to participate in family events, especially when adult children are no longer in the home. Make an effort to reach out to them and let them know you want them around. At the same time, do not expect invitations in return.
- Focus on parenting as a team. If your stepchildren are causing drama, your partner should back you up, request that your stepchildren show greater respect for you, and ask their children to treat you with kindness. Come up with a plan of attack for the next time a conflict escalates into disrespect and follow through on it.
- Create healthy boundaries for your stepchildren (if they are younger children).
- Get to know them as a person, not as a child. Often parents can have one view of older children that is quite different from how they perceive themselves. Instead of relying on your partner's assessment of their child's likes, dislikes, and personality, make an effort to get to know them on your own.
- Let them know that your relationship is a clean slate. No matter how challenging their behavior towards their parents has been in the past, if they were acting out or were struggling with keeping family rules, let your stepchild know their relationship with your starts with a clean slate.
- Make an effort to familiarize yourself with family traditions and help your new family keep them. In addition, make new family traditions that will help you bond and create a new sense of community and belonging.
- Be there physically for important events; more importantly, be there mentally. If your stepchild has an athletic event, a recital, or another event that they've put effort into, make sure you attend and that you are mentally present during the activity. No one likes to look into an audience while standing on stage and see faces turned down, lit up by smartphone screens.
- Be present. In addition to your physical presence in their lives, make an effort to be present whenever they engage in conversation with you. Make sure they understand they are important to

you.

- Have downtime so you can enjoy doing nothing together. Learn how to relax and take time as a family just being together without scheduled activities or pressure to do something worthwhile. Magic happens when families relax together. It creates a sense of ease and soothes away tension.

ASSIGNMENT 22

Find out what your stepchildren like to do. Ask them what activities they like or want to learn and write a list together. Use the box below

ASSIGNMENT 23

Find ways to incorporate their interests into your time with them. If you can, enroll them in activities they like, then support them in their interests.

ASSIGNMENT 24

Find time to spend one-on-one with each stepchild. Get ideas about what they want to do in your time together. Take notes below.

Stepchildren and Manipulation

All children can be manipulative in one way or another. Manipulation simply means "managing, using influence, or emotional reactions to achieve the desired result."

As infants, our children learn how to get their needs met by any means they can: crying, fussing, cooing, even smiling. An infant's motivations are simple to understand; they either want to please their parents by smiling, cooing, showing affection, etc., or alert the parents that they need to be fed, changed, comforted, etc. As children grow, they observe the behavior of their caregivers and use these observed behaviors to try to get their needs met. Parents continually reinforce our children's behavior and teach them how to get their needs met by how we respond to them. When we match their emotional intensity, even when inappropriate, we reinforce how they show emotions. We teach them to be manipulative by modeling manipulative behavior.

Let's look at an example of a potential conflict in your home.

Your stepchild wants to go to a friend's house to play. They ask politely if they can go. After some questioning, you discover they have not completed their homework. You, your partner, and your co-parent have all agreed your stepchildren must complete all homework assignments before they can go out to play. You remind them of the rule and deny their request until they finish their homework.

Now, the child has a choice. If they have learned that when asking doesn't get you what you want, you can put up a fight, scream, cry, or even lie to get results; they may choose to do those things. Or, they may have learned to ask your partner for permission to circumvent you and so choose to go to your partner.

While manipulative in nature, this type of misbehaving does not necessarily mean that the child is being manipulative. They are just mimicking behavior they have seen or repeating behavior that has been successful in the past. Classifying all of our stepchildren's misbehaviors or emotional outbursts as manipulation is an easy trap. Some children can be manipulative, and all are at specific points; however, we often misunderstand our stepchildren's motivations and misattribute them to a desire to manipulate us.

Children learn through experience how they can achieve their desired results using different behaviors. They are smart enough to know that each of their parents responds differently. They can be creative and determined to get what they want or need, which is an excellent skill when used in productive ways. We want our children to advocate for themselves, meet their needs, accomplish their goals, and stick up for their boundaries and values. However, when speaking up for your wants and needs isn't taught in a healthy manner, children can use it to manipulate others and quickly become a negative behavior, even though the child is only trying to meet their wants or needs. Fortunately, there are many resources available to parents whose children have learned to be manipulative to get their way and many ways to teach children prosocial skills they can use to have their needs met.

Many factors contribute to a child resorting to manipulative behavior to meet their needs. Children who engage in this behavior often just need extra love, support, and encouragement. When biological parents are separated, children struggle to learn how to navigate their way through two households with different parenting styles, different expectations, and different responsibilities. This huge life change is, at the very least, emotionally overwhelming and confusing for us as adults. For children, it shakes the very core of their life. Children of divorce need extra love, support, positive reinforcement, and loads of encouragement for positive, prosocial behaviors; they also need to know their boundaries and be reminded of those boundaries in a healthy, loving way.

You can count on children to test your boundaries; how you react will help them understand what you expect of them and what you will and will not tolerate. It is up to us, as adults, to provide appropriate boundaries. When we fail to do so, children learn how to manipulate and get what they want in ways we don't like.

First, let's look at some easy ways to identify and stop the pattern of manipulation.

1. Become aware of your stepchild's manipulative behaviors. Do your stepchildren act sad when they don't get what they want because they sense you are afraid of hurting their feelings? Do they use the divide and conquer technique, pitting you against your partner or co-parent by lying or intentionally withholding information? Do they scream at you to trigger your emotional responses, things like "I hate you! You're not my real mom!" or "My other dad lets me do whatever I want?" Once you have identified their manipulative behaviors, you can respond the next time they attempt to manipulate you in an appropriately loving but firm way to reinforce your rules and set the standard for acceptable behavior. For example, if your child is pushing back on bedtime and using guilt to trigger an emotional response, "I never get to spend time with my daddy. I miss him!" You can respond appropriately, "I'm sorry, I know it's hard to have your daddy gone at work. We will make sure you can spend an hour with him after work tomorrow, just the two of you. Right now, though, it's still bedtime, and your daddy will come and tuck you in."

2. Be aware of your own triggers. If your parents neglected your emotional wellbeing and you are very sensitive to your stepchild's emotional wellbeing, hearing them say something like "You don't love me" might trigger an emotional reaction for you and compel you to bend your own rules. Or maybe they use a certain tone of voice or look that sets you off. When you understand your triggers, you are empowered to resist allowing others to push your buttons.

3. Decide, with your partner, your parenting style and principles. Many of us were raised in unhealthy environments without a positive parental role model. Others were lucky to have great parents who taught us positive life lessons. However you were raised, the good news is you get to decide how you will parent. When you approach parenting as a role you play, and you define ahead of time how you want to play that role, you are empowered to make better decisions when your stepchildren try to manipulate you.

4. Encourage communication. I encourage the regular sharing of needs and healthy communication during everyday moments. Creating an established pattern of successful communication helps reduce the chances of an emotional breakdown over unmet needs. When your stepchild is upset, it may become difficult for them to communicate their needs in a positive way. A quiet tone of voice and slower speech can help our stepchildren de-escalate when emotionally overwhelmed during intense situations. When you use a gentle, calm, slower pace when speaking to your upset children, you are also more likely to remain in control of your emotions.

5. Give them the benefit of the doubt. No one wants to have their motives questioned all the time. Your stepchild might have behaviors that you disagree with, but that doesn't make them naughty or bad; they just need to be shown a different way to get their needs met. Most children respond exceptionally well to patience, kindness, respect, and love. Show your stepchild that you believe in them and all their goodness. You'll be amazed at what happens when you respond in love.

6. Take care of yourself. We react much more calmly when we are not over-stressed. Make sure you take time to take care of your own needs so you will have more patience and can react in a positive, kind way when parenting challenges arrive.

Sometimes we are helpless to reinforce positive, prosocial behaviors when our stepchildren are not under our direct care; this is especially true when a manipulative co-parent may be sabotaging our efforts to raise healthy, emotionally well-adjusted children. They may be reinforcing or even encouraging inappropriate, unhealthy behaviors. When this happens, you can only go back to what you can control and what is out of your control. You can't make your co-parent act like an adult or control what they reinforce while you're stepchildren are in their home; however, you can teach your stepchildren how to get their needs met in appropriate ways, provide positive reinforcement, safety, and clear house rules with natural consequences when they are in your home.

Manipulative behaviors might be especially present in children with oppositional defiant disorders. Children in a loyalty bind also tend to show more manipulative behavior. If this is the case for your stepchildren, your first reaction might be to double-down trying to control their behavior in your home. Beware, in these circumstances, this type of reaction will backfire. You cannot control your stepchild's behavior, but you can control how you behave. Take a step back, and assess the situation before deciding how to proceed. Ask yourself if you want to stick to the house rules as they are currently established? Are your house rules truly reasonable for this child's situation? How can you help them feel loved and validated? If the child is being used as a tool to wreak havoc in your home, do you want to disengage from raising them? Do you want to take them to therapy so they can learn how to talk about their feelings and have a safe place to do so? What you decide to do is up to you and your partner, and should include both considerations about what's best for the children and what's best for you as a couple.

Remember, children are still growing and learning, and their parents have taught them, intentionally or not, how to behave. They may not know what manipulation is or that they're being manipulative; they just know that what they're doing has worked for them in the past. It is up to our partners and us to show them a better way.

ASSIGNMENT 25

Think about something that your stepchild/stepchildren are doing that you feel is manipulative. What need do you think they're trying to fill?

ASSIGNMENT 26

How would you like your stepchild/stepchildren to act to get their needs met?

ASSIGNMENT 27

How can you help your stepchildren feel safe enough to address and change their behavior?

Your Partner, Your Ally

Before we close out the section on building a relationship with your stepchildren, let's talk about your most significant ally - your partner. Your partner has a massive impact on your relationship with their children. Suppose your partner introduced you without first talking to their children. In that case, it will be challenging to build a relationship with your stepchildren until you can establish some expectations of how they should interact with you. A successful, mutually fulfilling relationship with your stepchildren always begins with a framework for the children to help them understand how they should behave towards you.

One way to establish this framework is to have your partner let the children know that what you say carries the same weight as what they say. Ideally, your co-parent will back this up. (Most of us, however, are in less-than-ideal situations with their co-parent, thus the need for this workbook.)

If your partner is unwilling to set expectations, talk with them about why. Is it because they're reluctant to set any expectations or limits with their children? Are they afraid of losing time or their relationship with their children? Is there parental alienation happening from your co-parent? If your partner isn't helping you or supporting you, it's challenging to be happy or fulfilled as a stepparent. When your partner does support you and takes what you want into account, your relationship functions better, and you have more success as a stepparent.

All relationships experience difficulties, even more so when you add in the challenges of your partner's ex and children. I am fortunate; Chris is EXTREMELY supportive of me. He doesn't always understand why I do what I do and what's important to me, but he almost always comes around and supports me in what I want. I say almost always because although he is very supportive, we have different opinions about homework, screen time, and smartphone access.

If your partner is not as supportive as you need, talk to them and seek out counseling, if necessary. Sometimes, all our efforts to communicate effectively with our partners fail. Especially if they refuse to work towards understanding what they need to do or why you're struggling with co-parenting, or how their behavior undermines your relationship with your stepchildren; if this happens, you will need to decide whether the relationship with your partner is working for you, or if you want to make that relationship work. Only you can make that decision, and it's not a decision to make lightly.

If your partner is willing to change and support you, help them understand how they can help and what you would like your relationship with your stepchildren to function. Let them know what boundaries and family rules are important to you. Encourage them to give positive reinforcement when your stepchildren follow the established boundaries and rules. Let them know how happy and grateful you are to be part of the family and how much you appreciate them. Also, continue to work on your relationship with your stepchildren so your partner can see you're making an effort to be part of the family and love or like their children.

Building A Relationship With The Co-Parent

To have a relationship with your co-parent, they first have to want to have a relationship with you. In some cases, but not always, a relationship with your co-parent is a bad idea, especially when they don't like you, aren't in a place where they want to hear your name or see you, or won't speak to you. Biological parents often only want to communicate and deal with their former partner because legally, only your partner can make decisions for the children. No matter how much you want a good relationship with your co-parent, you cannot force someone into a relationship when the feeling isn't mutual; this applies to both co-parents and stepchildren. That's the bad news. The good news is that many co-parenting relationships can become less contentious over time.

My relationship with my stepdaughters' mom has changed over time. In the beginning, I felt insecure and jealous, like I had something to prove. Even though she was nice to me during the times we were required to interact, like baptisms or school events, I now see that I made our interactions more difficult because I didn't have the skills I needed to interact with her in a healthy way. However, over the past few years, our relationship has evolved. While I wouldn't say we're to the point of wanting to spend our free time together, we can talk when and we do get along okay. Like all relationships, ours has evolved. My stepdaughters' mom has recently moved away, and I no longer have contact with her since the girls are grown. However, I know we will have contact in the future when the girls have big life events, like graduations and weddings. I hold hope that we can continue to get along when this happens.

Building a relationship with your co-parent requires the same effort as building a relationship with anyone else. Still, it may require a little more delicacy, patience, and time. The most important part of building a productive relationship with your co-parent is to help the children see their parents getting along as much as possible. It might be difficult, and it will take time, but in the end, the effort is well worth it!

Involve Your Partner

As much as you don't want to think about it; your partner has an established relationship and complex history with their ex. As you begin to build a relationship with your co-parent, involve your partner and ask for advice. They will know from their history together how their ex will react, what their triggers are, and how best to work and communicate with them. If they say that their ex isn't willing or ready to have a relationship with you, respect that. Don't try to push the relationship, and definitely don't think you can change your co-parent's mind just because you are a good person. Let them set their boundaries for you and respect them.

Start Small and Take It Slow

If your co-parent is willing to have a relationship with you, start by taking small steps to get to know them on neutral ground. Ask if they want to get coffee so you can talk, or suggest they come with you to the park the next time you take the children. Take notice of small things they do and express your appreciation to them. In the beginning, keep the focus on the great or cute things your stepchildren are doing to build on a ground of common interests. Hopefully, your co-parent may start to see everything you do for your stepchildren over time. As they begin to understand that you love their children and see you as an ally, you can learn how to get along for your stepchildren's sake and make things easier for everyone involved. Even though you're going to have disagreements and the occasional conflicts, because you're human and imperfect, and you will do things that you regret, you can keep trying to improve your relationship with your co-parent. Your shared experiences will help you create a cooperative relationship rather than a competitive or contentious one.

It can easily backfire if you overstep your boundaries by suggesting parenting tips to your co-parent. Instead of making assumptions about their motivations behind specific actions, ask kindly, then you can both learn to answer honestly. Any criticism or complaints of the co-parent should be reserved for therapy, talking to friends, or problem solving with your partner. Hopefully, as you keep going in your co-parenting relationship, you learn how to forgive and give each other grace.

In my work as a school psychologist, I've seen hostile parents respond well when they understand you're on their side and that you want the best for their child. As you begin your relationship with your co-parent, let them get to know you and your good intentions for their children. It's ok for them to know you're imperfect and that you make mistakes. Being honest and human helps build relationships of trust. Let them know how great you think their children are, how you are proud of their efforts in their chosen activities like sports or dance or at whatever they're creating. Every parent wants to hear good things about their children and that they are loved and protected by the adults responsible for them. When your co-parent knows you see the good in their children, it goes a long way to soften their heart towards you.

ASSIGNMENT 28

Think about whether you want to have a relationship with your co-parent. Journal your thoughts.

ASSIGNMENT 29

Talk to your partner about whether they feel that you could start to build a relationship with their ex. What do they think could be good about you having a relationship with their ex? What could make things complicated? Make notes below.

ASSIGNMENT 30

If you decide to build a relationship with your co-parent, determine what you want to do with them. If you feel it's best for you not to build a relationship right now, move on to the next chapter.

CHAPTER 6

When Conflict Arises

The Importance of Therapy

Therapy saved my life. In my late teens and early twenties, I was a mess. I had an eating disorder, major depressive disorder, and I struggled with almost daily suicidal thoughts. I hadn't ever heard of thinking errors. I didn't know that the way I was interpreting my life situations and interactions with other people made my life harder. Two therapists helped me through this challenging time, and now, several more therapists have helped me improve myself, strengthen my marriage, and find happiness.

As an individual, therapy can help you see how your current behaviors and thinking patterns are, or are not, working in your favor. Therapists help you understand how inherited paradigms from your family of origin affect how you interact and react to life events. They also help you learn how to identify and reflect on how you might be misinterpreting certain situations.

As a stepparent, therapy is a valuable tool to help you learn how to analyze and release the negative emotions and experiences that often accompany the role of a stepparent. Your therapist will help you to reality check, solve problems, learn new coping skills, and learn how to communicate better with your loved ones.

Many people go to therapy to learn coping skills. Coping skills are different from self-care. Self-care is what we do for daily/weekly wellness maintenance. Coping skills help us manage our emotions and well-being during stress or crisis. Your therapist is a neutral third party who will listen to you as you vent to help you see your blind spots and objectively help you figure out helpful strategies.

Couples Therapy

When Chris and I were dating, I was in a big hurry to get married. He wanted to take his time and make sure that he wasn't rushing into marriage for several reasons, one of which was that he wanted to make sure he was over his ex-wife. I didn't understand that then, but I appreciate the wisdom now. Chris took the time he needed to allow him time to work through the inevitable feelings that come from divorce and make sure I wasn't a "rebound" relationship. Even with that, we still had a hard time adjusting to marriage. As most people do, we have different communication styles, behavioral patterns, coping methods, and interpretations of events based on our individual experiences. Sometimes, I'm amazed that anyone gets married and stays married because we're all raised so differently from each other, and it can be hard to overcome those differences. Couples therapy can be a huge asset in the success of your marriage.

Couples therapy can help many couples through difficulties in their relationship and can be particularly helpful in a stepfamily, especially if you find a therapist who specializes in blended families. In Chapters Two and Four, we learned about how we all bring functionality or dysfunctionality from our family of origin into marriage, including family traditions, styles of communication, unwritten family rules, beliefs, emotional responses, and assumptions. It can also include trauma responses from our past. When you consider how programmed we are by our families of origin and how this programming differs between families, it's no wonder we sometimes need an intermediary to help us communicate and problem-solve more effectively. Additionally, people from failed marriages often need counseling to help them work through the issues that caused their divorce or the problems that came about because of their divorce.

Couples therapy is a great way to help you figure out how you, both individually and as a couple, can improve your communication, identify limiting beliefs and actions and determine how they affect your relationship and at what cost. Therapy helps you become aware so you can choose to do better. One caveat is that therapy, like anything else, will give you only results that you work towards; therapy won't work if you or your partner aren't willing to be open, honest, and ready to change as you face your issues.

The importance of getting help in your marriage cannot be overstated. If your partner doesn't want to go to therapy, start by going yourself. The things you learn and how you change can impact your partner and your children or stepchildren. If your partner is willing to go, that's huge! Willingness to go to therapy demonstrates that they are open to change and trust that the relationship and the therapeutic process will work. Whether you participate in therapy together or are going at it alone, having someone to talk to and help you sort through your relationship is one of the best ways to learn how to be happier and more peaceful.

ASSIGNMENT 1

Talk to your partner about going to therapy. What are their thoughts and feelings on it?

ASSIGNMENT 2

Go online to the website for your insurance or to a support group you trust and ask for recommendations on a therapist. Make notes below, if needed.

Dealing With Parental Alienation or High-Conflict Co-Parents

The most difficult co-parents to deal with are those who are high-conflict and engage in parental alienation. Parental alienation is when one biological parent actively tries to separate and alienate the child from their other biological parent. Parental alienation may also include your co-parent attempting to alienate your stepchildren from you. Parental alienation often happens when the alienating parent is mentally ill, but this is not always the case.

Usually, an alienating parent is narcissistic. People with narcissistic personalities will always feel that you or your partner have wronged them. An alienating co-parent will continually attempt to sabotage any attempts you make to connect with your partner or stepchildren. No matter what you do, how much you love the kids, how good of a person you are, an alienating co-parent will not ever see anything you do in the correct light; their actions and feelings have absolutely nothing to do with you.

Sometimes, in the absence of mental illness, parental alienation is a conscious effort to cause pain or obtain justice for some perceived wrong. Parental alienation may include purposefully withholding information about parent-teacher conferences, school events, doctor appointments, church or sports activities, important family events, etc., to make you and your partner look bad. It may also include lying: to you, your partner, or the children to get them to take sides. Frequently, parents who alienate children were abusive to their partners when they were together, so counseling for your partner will be helpful. Suppose parental alienation is happening in your family. In that case, it is essential for you to use the mindset and coping skills you have, or that you will learn in therapy, and discuss appropriate responses and actions with your partner.

Most children manipulated by a parent's attempts to alienate the other parent tend to develop a loyalty bind. A loyalty bind is when a child feels like they must choose one parent over the other.

Loyalty binds can cause children to feel like they're not allowed to love both parents, and they have to side with one of their parents during arguments. Developmentally, younger children don't understand or believe that their parents lie to or mislead them, so they have no reason not to believe the alienating parent.

You can attempt to avoid a loyalty bind wherever possible by showing your stepchild love and support and not making them choose between their parents. If it's developmentally appropriate, have a conversation with your stepchild to let them know that you love and support them, and they don't have to choose between their parents.

It can feel like a personal attack when your stepchild is in a loyalty bind because your stepchild has rejected you; however, keep in mind that your stepchild's actions are not about you. Children have a subconscious need to protect their parents because if their parents aren't safe, the children aren't safe. When given a choice, most children will choose their biological parents over their stepparents, and it's important to remember that their choice isn't actually about you—it's an innate biological drive for their safety.

I have witnessed several cases of parental alienation. In general, the behavior doesn't always start as a conscious effort to alienate the child/children from their other parent and the stepparent. However, after some time has passed, the alienating parent's behaviors intensify or become intentional, and the co-parents get sucked in and want to defend themselves. When you have someone in your life who is constantly trying to tear you down, criticizes everything you do, or who tells your stepchildren negative things about you, the knee-jerk reaction is to engage with them or defend yourself, which is not helpful for you, your partner, or your relationship with your stepchildren. As adults, we have to learn how to deal with frustration, pain, hurt, betrayal, and defensiveness, all while parenting our stepchildren in a healthy way, which is SO DIFFICULT. Therapy is no longer optional when parental alienation happens in your family; it is essential.

Should you go back to court?

It is difficult to prove that parental alienation is happening for several reasons:
- Most of the evidence of this type of behavior is hearsay,
- Children cannot be called upon to testify against their parents,
- Video or audio recordings of what a child reports to the other parent are not allowed in court because what the children say could be heavily influenced by either parent
- The court can't, or won't monitor what your co-parent is saying about you or your partner.

Family court systems typically don't provide a lot of recourse for parental alienation; however, they offer some helpful options to limit the damage this type of behavior causes. They may require your partner and co-parent to attend co-parent coordination meetings or participate in parenting classes or counseling. You can request that all communication goes through a medium a mediator can read, like

Our Family Wizard, Talking Parents, AppClose, or other options. Some of these also have a calendar feature; some have options to track and reimburse expenses. Your partner may also want to protect themself against any allegations at pickups and dropoffs by asking to have a third party present. If you choose to take an alienating parent back to court to help resolve the conflict, get recommendations for lawyers in your area who specialize in parental alienation to ensure the best possible outcome.

Other High-Conflict Problems

Parental alienation is not the only high-conflict situation in blended families; it is just one of the more common ones. Examples of high-conflict parenting behaviors include:
*   Verbally or physically abusive behavior at pickups and dropoffs,
*   Refusing to give the other parent their court-ordered parenting time,
*   Abusing the court system by taking the other parent to court constantly for what appears to be no reason,
*   Making false reports to child protective services,
*   Demanding more child-support than the court orders,
*   Lying about costs of daycare to make the other parent pay more.

The following are examples of behaviors that are NOT high-conflict:
*   Setting boundaries,
*   Insisting on communication only between the biological parents,
*   Exercising the first right of refusal if their ex is at work and unavailable to be with the children.

Sometimes as stepparents, we can be high-conflict when our expectations and beliefs aren't appropriate for the circumstances. Most people don't want to be high-conflict; they just want to do what they want and have as much time as possible with their children or stepchildren. When we deal well with our negative emotions about co-parenting and try to resolve or stay out of conflicts, we create more peace and balance in our lives, relationships, and stepparenting, regardless of what our co-parent is doing.

ASSIGNMENT 3

Think about what your co-parent is doing that you feel is high-conflict. Journal your thoughts.

ASSIGNMENT 4

Take a hard look at your behavior. Are you doing anything that contributes to a high-conflict co-parenting relationship? Journal your answers.

ASSIGNMENT 5

Discuss your co-parenting with your partner. How is it going? Are there things you both want to change? Journal your findings below.

ASSIGNMENT 6

If you believe parental alienation is happening, talk to your partner and decide on a plan to handle it. Consider the personality of your co-parent and figure out a way to address them or to parallel parent.

Disengage From Your Partner's Ex or Children

There will be many times in your relationship when you will have to step back both from the children and from your partner's ex; recognizing when it's time to take a breather can help you be happier and have more peace. When we come into our new families, it is natural for us as stepparents to want to make meaningful contributions; however, when we do this, we sometimes step outside of our role as stepparents, which can cause problems. While each of our roles as stepparents is by necessity different, we can do things to stay within the boundaries of our role, which will help us disengage to create balance and peace.

Disengagement is different from withdrawing. When we disengage, we detach ourselves from the outcome of a situation to show respect, love, and trust. It is not running away, getting angry, shutting down, or blaming your partner or their children. My favorite phrase that sums up disengagement is "Not my circus, not my monkeys." Even though you are part of your family, your role as a stepparent may mean you are not responsible for your partner's children, although you can love them and help raise them. You don't have anything to prove to yourself, your partner, stepchildren, or co-parent. Knowing your role in parenting your stepchildren is crucial.

It may be helpful to define parenting in context here to help further your understanding of disengagement. Parenting and parental responsibility are two different terms. Parenting means more than just daily care of the children, like feeding, clothing, and helping them get to their day-to-day activities. As a stepparent, you most likely are involved in these parts of your family's daily life. As a stepparent, you will likely be involved in your stepchildren's lives just as intimately as your partner is; however, this is where conflict can arise because you, as the stepparent, have little authority when it comes to enforcing discipline or consequences.

Biological parents also have parental responsibility, which means they are the primary providers of their children's financial, emotional, and mental support. It also means they are responsible for determining major life decisions for their children, defining consequences for misbehavior, and enforcing family rules. These primary parental responsibilities should fall squarely on the shoulders of your partner and their ex unless the ex is absent, unable, or unwilling to do so. In this circumstance, your role as a stepparent should be discussed and defined with your partner so you can avoid overstepping your role, which can end badly.

Overstepping Your Role

There are many ways stepparents can overstep their role. In my experience, many stepmoms try to take charge of communication between their partner and their partner's ex, which is a prime example of overstepping and is an excellent place to begin disengaging and detaching. Your partner and their ex have established their style of communication. You may not like it, agree with it, or find it effective, but you are overstepping in your partnership if you try to change or take charge of their communication. If the communication between your partner and their ex needs a buffer, apps can facilitate this. Stay as far away from managing their communication as you possibly can. Your partner and co-parent are responsible for raising the children, and they need to be able to talk to each other without interference. Although you may feel like it's easier for you than your partner to communicate with your co-parent, your co-parent may feel like you are stepping in when it is not your place.

Discipline and enforcing rules and boundaries is another area where stepparents commonly overstep. For example, maybe things are going fine in your blended family. You have gotten into a groove, and you become comfortable being an authority figure in your home and disciplining your stepchildren. One of your stepchildren does something that you do not find acceptable, so you set a boundary or reinforce an existing boundary. Suddenly, your co-parent blows up at you, accusing you of overstepping your place. You feel like this reaction came out of nowhere; however, resentment and frustration have been building for your co-parent for a while because they feel like you have been trying to take their place as a primary parent rather than as a secondary parent or friend/ally your stepchildren.

Another area where parents, co-parents, or stepparents can easily overstep their role is when they attempt to set rules for the children at their other parent's home, which shifts the control from one parent to another.

Many of us are triggered when other's try to take our control away; which can cause us to double-down our efforts control our own lives (and maybe even try to exert control in the lives of our children when we feel our self-control is threatened), this is one of those times when we need to practice disengagement. Let me share an example of a situation that happened in our family.

Chris and I once lived in a house with a community pool. My husband, co-parent, and I come from a strict religious background, with particular guidelines about Sunday conduct. My co-parent set a rule for my stepdaughters that they couldn't swim at our house on Sundays, citing the rules of the religion, even though this religion does not have a specific rule that forbids swimming on Sunday. Even if it did, my co-parent overstepped by trying to place limits on my stepdaughter's activities while they were in our home, during our parenting time. Naturally, when I heard about the restriction, I became very upset.

When I calmed down, I understood that I needed to disengage. I gave myself time before I responded to think about how involved I wanted to be and what type of reaction would be appropriate. I knew that her desire to limit her daughter's activities was really about her expectations, not about me and what we allowed at our house. Not my circus, not my monkeys.

My eldest stepdaughter moved in with us full-time about a year ago. Since then, the practice I had disengaging from my co-parent has been very helpful in my relationship with my stepdaughter. At first, I saw her moving in as an opportunity to help her undo a lot of the negative programming she received as a child. However, the more I got to know her through day-to-day interactions, the more I realized that she was not looking for or in need of another parent because she already had a great parent, my husband! My step-daughter needed someone to love her and support her, which is entirely appropriate for me to do as her stepmother.

Even though I care about my stepdaughters and know from life and professional experience what they can do to make life easier, it is not my place to force any of what I know onto them. What they need and want are very different from what I want for them, and it is not my place to try to change them. I have to disengage to have a productive, mutually respectful, positive relationship. I'm able to talk with them about things that they like and don't like, their wishes and hopes, and they're more honest and open with me than they have been in the past. When done correctly and with love, disengaging leads to a better relationship with your stepchildren and your partner.

When To Disengage

Stepparents disengage from primary parenting by stepping back from making decisions about discipline, rules, and boundaries to allow the biological parents to take responsibility for parenting their children, your level of disengagement will, of necessity, vary from child to child. Disengaging will look significantly different when you consider a child's age; there is a big difference between disengaging when you have a three-year-old in your home vs. a 19-year-old. An older teen can function on their own, for the most part, and doesn't need you to parent them; they need you to be a supportive authority figure who provides love, acceptance, and friendship. If you have a younger child, who needs more supervision and parental guidance, disengagement will look more like supporting your partner as they fulfill their primary parental responsibilities as you nurture, support, watch over, and care for the young child's daily needs. Remember, your goal is to remove your expectations and inappropriate control over your stepchildren, not neglect them.

Disengagement does not mean ignoring your stepchildren or your co-parent. When you disengage, you still have a relationship. Disengaging from primary parenting means that you do not take responsibility for your stepchildren's actions, discipline, appointments, etc. When you disengage, you allow your stepchildren's biological parents to be their primary parents. As an outsider, it's easy for us to want to step into a situation and see what needs to be fixed. However, people don't want to be fixed; they just want us to accept and love them and give them the support they need. Disengagement also shows your partner that you trust them to parent their children, a crucial component to a healthy partnership/ family dynamic.

Disengagement is a hot topic in stepparenting circles, and it's not one everyone agrees with or understands in the same way. Disengagement is harder for women because we tend to be more involved in the day-to-day management of the household and children, and we tend to become emotionally invested in the outcome of our familial responsibilities. Generally speaking, women are socialized to be primary caregivers, and that's no different in stepparenting, which is why figuring out your role in your blended family is so important.

Even though most men are not raised to be primary caregivers, men also struggle with proactively disengaging from their stepchildren and co-parent when their partners want them to step in more with raising the children. As a stepfather, disengaging from disciplinary decisions is especially important when the co-parent is still heavily involved in the children's lives.

If I could go back and change anything in my marriage to Chris, I would have had more conversations with him about my new role as a stepmother. I would have asked Chris what his expectations were and what support he needed from me. I would have talked to my co-parent about how I could help her, without overstepping my role. Unfortunately, at the time, I had thinking errors, insecurities, and uncertainties that caused a lot of blocks when it came to talking with her. Now that I know better, I am passing my wisdom on to you. Even though these types of conversations are challenging, they're an essential part of creating a productive and happy blended family. Disengagement is also critical in preventing stepparent burnout.

A good therapist or stepparent coach will help you figure out what to let go of and how to support your partner in their role as the primary parent, which will help you maintain appropriate boundaries and teach by example those around you how to do the same.

ASSIGNMENT 7

Journal how you feel about disengaging from your stepchildren. What do you like about it? What reservations do you have about disengagement?

ASSIGNMENT 8

Talk to your partner about how you could disengage from stepparenting. What are their thoughts on it? Take notes in the box below.

ASSIGNMENT 9

Decide on one way you can disengage to benefit your mental health and figure out a way to do that.

Everyone Is the Hero of Their Own Story

Good intentions - we all have them. An outside observer may not understand our good intentions, but most of us sincerely want to make decisions and conduct our lives in an honorable way. We all see ourselves as "the good guy" or the hero in our life stories.

Over the past thirteen years, as I have worked with blended families, biological parents, and stepparents, I have seen one constant: we all believe we're doing the right things for the right reasons.

The formative experiences in our life, the way we interact with and relate to our family and community, and the way we interpret our interactions and events contribute significantly to how we conduct ourselves in our relationships. Not one stepparent or biological parent I've worked with has believed that their actions were done with malicious intent. Consistently, they think that their decisions and actions are only to serve and protect themselves and their children's best interests and well-being.

Keeping this perspective in mind can help us view our co-parent's behaviors with more empathy, or at least more patience. Understanding that our co-parents are acting in a way that they think will make them and their children happy or that their decisions allow them to feel like they're protecting their children enables us to change our perspective and actions.

We are the only ones who know why we do the things we do, and we tend to judge ourselves based on our intentions; however, we also tend to judge others based on their actions or the outcome of their behavior. It's hard for us to understand other people's motives when all we can see is how their behavior affects us.

For example, have you ever taken interaction with your co-parent personally? News flash, it's not about you! It's about them, their motivations, their intentions, and how they see the world around them! There are exceptions to this "good intentions rule," especially when your co-parent has a significant mental illness, is narcissistic, or if they are hell-bent on revenge; but in most situations, your co-parent is probably trying to do their best to raise their kids and have a happy life.

None of us can reliably read the mind of another person, so it's easy to believe our co-parent is intentionally doing or saying things to hurt us, but we can try to see things from their perspective. Even if you think your co-parent is out of their mind, what would change for you if you tried to see something they do from their perspective? Can you imagine yourself in their story where they're trying to do their best? Would seeing things from their perspective help you understand their point of view?

Raising children isn't about who is right or wrong; it's about raising emotionally healthy children. I know this is a massive mindset shift, and it involves questioning a lot of what you believe about people and why they act the way they do.

Sometimes parents hurt their kids, even if they see themselves as heroes. They can't see past their perspective to empathize with others, including their children. However, we have the power to change our own perspectives and try to understand others' motivations, which helps us be more proactive and peaceful co-parents. At the very least, when you change your perspective to give others the benefit of the doubt, it will help you to develop patience and empathy when we interact with our co-parent.

ASSIGNMENT 10

Think of a recent situation where your co-parent did something that bothered you. How did you interpret their actions?

ASSIGNMENT 11

Looking back at that particular situation, is there a way you can change the way you view what they did so it isn't about you or so that hurts you less?

ASSIGNMENT 12

How would you respond differently in that example if you didn't personalize it?

Have Empathy, Show Grace

Empathy is a critical skill in any relationship, whether it's with your partner, your stepchild/ stepchildren, your parents or bio kids, your co-parent, or yourself. Having empathy for everyone involved in co-parenting can be challenging to say the least. As a stepparent, you've come into a family with existing rules, patterns of interaction, traditions, ways of communicating, and parenting styles, and these may be SO different from how things were in your family of origin. The first few years can be tough; in fact, it takes an average of five to seven years for a family to blend. Those first years can be extremely difficult, and that's just taking your new family into account. When you add your co-parent to this mix, you may feel unheard, unappreciated, and unloved, and when you're in that space, it's difficult to show empathy to others. It can be challenging to come from a place of love and understand others' perspectives when we're feeling triggered. Taking care of yourself during this time is critical, as is making sure you're emotionally healthy and mature enough to handle any stepparenting challenges.

When you enter into a relationship with your partner, you realize that they're not perfect, and what you hear about their previous relationship is only one side of the story. Your co-parent has a different story to tell, and the truth of why the relationship failed is likely somewhere between the two sides. Marcus Aurelius said, "Everything we hear is an opinion, not a fact. Everything we see is a perspective, not the truth." Keeping this in mind when co-parenting can be very helpful.

Most people are not intentionally malicious. However, there seems to be a higher incidence of maliciousness and revenge in families with divorce and co-parenting than in the general population due to hurt feelings, lack of control, and the need to "get even" with an ex.

Developing empathy for someone trying to bring you down or hurt their ex (or even the children) requires a high level of self-awareness and emotional IQ, much more than having empathy for someone who is unintentionally hurting those around you.

When I started to show empathy for my co-parent, everything changed. I detached from her actions, stopped making assumptions about what she was doing and why, and just dealt with what was in my control in the here and now. I showed her kindness instead of resentment or apathy. I became so much happier when I stopped focusing on what was out of my control and started focusing on what I could do to influence my family positively.

When we make assumptions about the intentions of others, it doesn't hurt the other person, but it poisons us. It makes us unhappy, makes us ready to take offense at everything they do, and causes us to focus on them more often than we want to. When we can let go of judging others, we have more room in our lives for the things that make us happy. Also, our assumptions about other people are often wrong. When we metaphorically put ourselves in their shoes and understand their intentions, we find our perspective changes. I understand this is not always the case, but if we can show empathy, at the very least, that will make us better and happier people.

Tracy Poizner, who founded The Essential Stepmom podcast and the Spectacular Stepmom Facebook group, points out that all women struggle with feelings that they are not good enough—like they are failing at being a good wife or mom, etc.—these feelings are magnified in situations of divorce.

A biological mom may feel like her ex is better off now that she isn't his partner. She might perceive him as a better partner and father and happier and more successful because she is no longer weighing him down or feel like her co-parent is a better mother than she is. All of these beliefs are subjective. Her ex might be a better partner and father now, but he is in a relationship that better suits him. Her children might be happier now, but that is most likely due to less contention in the home. Her co-parent might be a wonderful mother, but that has nothing to do with her ability to be a good mother. All of her insecurities are due to her perception.

Showing empathy is critical to developing a peaceful relationship between co-parents. When we understand and respect that our co-parent has experienced trauma and is grieving the loss of their marriage, missing their children, and feeling insecure or jealous, we can show empathy (not pity). If you look at the perspective that many fear their co-parent is doing a better job at parenting than they, then the way that our co-parent acts begin to make sense.

I'm a big believer in the Golden Rule and the Law of Attraction. When we treat people kindly and with grace and respect, that's what we get in return (again, for the most part—if you're dealing with someone who is narcissistic/alienating, you can treat them well, and they'll just hurt you over and over again).

Whether or not your co-parent reciprocates your goodwill, focus on what is in your control. Go back to why you're doing this; it's not so that others will treat you well, but because you know that when you maintain your integrity and act from a place of empathy and healthy boundaries, you'll be happier in your life.

ASSIGNMENT 13

Think about the beliefs you have about others. How do you usually view and treat them?

ASSIGNMENT 14

Think about your co-parent. How do you feel about them? How do you treat them? Do you think they need empathy? Journal how you can show greater empathy to your co-parent.

ASSIGNMENT 15

What thoughts/beliefs do you have about your stepchildren, their behavior, manners, and how they treat you? Does this affect how you treat them?

ASSIGNMENT 16

Do you want to change how you interact with anyone around you? Or do you feel like you're doing well at showing empathy?

Well-Meaning People

People can say the worst things sometimes. They mean well, or they think they're trying to help, but can say things that are not helpful, hurt our feelings, or cause negative reactions in us. Some of the most frequent hurtful things people say to stepparents are:
- "You knew what you were getting into when you married/started dating/got into a relationship with someone who had kids."
- "You should love your stepchildren like they're your own."
- "When you married your partner, you married her/his children"
- "Well, you're not their real mom/dad, so…"
- "They're not your real children."
- "They're not my grandchildren."

Most people don't mean to be rude or hurt our feelings, but they also don't think about what they say and how we might receive it. Stepparents aren't the only group that hears thoughtless remarks, but that doesn't make us feel any better when people say these things. They might know what it's like to be a stepparent, but they don't know what it is like to be a stepparent in your blended family. They don't know how hard you try to love your stepchildren. They don't stop to think that stepparenting, like all parenting, isn't predictable or a straight path and that no matter how prepared we might feel, things will always come up that challenge us.

Parenting, in general, requires thick skin, but stepparenting requires an extra measure of toughness, especially when people are being hyper-critical and thoughtless. Unfortunately, these unhelpful and hurtful comments don't always come from outside observers; most often, they come from our parents, family of origin, partners, in-laws, stepchildren, or co-parents.

My first experience with well-meaning people was about two years after I married Chris. I was discussing motherhood with my father-in-law, and I confided in him some of the difficulties I was experiencing as a stepparent. He said, "You knew what you were getting into, marrying someone with kids," and I kind of lost it on him. I angrily told him that no one ever knows what they're getting into when they get married, let alone when they become a stepparent. When you make a decision, any decision, you make it based on what you know, then hope for the best. Even with all the help available to stepparents with the internet, books, support groups, etc., adjusting to life as a stepparent is still difficult. Some things come up that no one could have predicted. Things come up that your partner is used to and didn't mention to you because she/he/they are used to it, so it didn't cross their mind.

We can't control what other people say to us. We can't control whether or not they understand the scope of stepparenting. They may be insensitive to our unique situation; they may not know what it means to take on kids that aren't biologically yours, who don't live with you all the time, and with whom you may not have a bond.

We can control our thoughts, beliefs, responses, and reactions. When someone says something thoughtless to us, especially when they mean well, we have the power to decide whether we have the emotional strength and energy to respond to them positively, educate them, just smile and nod, or walk away without answering. We can also choose to educate people in our social circles about stepparenting and what we need when it's not what they're giving.

How you respond to people is 100% up to you, and your response will vary from day to day and person to person, depending on your relationship with them. Knowing what I know now, I would be calmer if I could go back in time to when my father-in-law made his remark; I now understand it wasn't a judgment of me, my abilities, or my value; it was about his perceptions and his lack of experience as a stepparent.

What other people say about our stepparenting isn't a factual description of our experiences or even us as people; it's just their belief and perception based on their observations and experience or lack thereof. When you truly realize that what others say is more about them than it is about you, you can disengage from their negativity and judgments and make the best choices for your life.

The process of learning how to disengage from well-meaning people takes time. As with anything new, your commitment to your new beliefs will be tested with each unique experience and relationship. All that means is that you may feel like you've mastered responding instead of reacting, but when someone close to you is thoughtless, you may still react.

Allow yourself to make mistakes and show yourself grace when you do. Apologize if you hurt others when they hurt you. One of my favorite sayings is "Hurt people hurt people," meaning that when we're hurt, we're more likely to hurt others. We all struggle; we all have our inner battles and beliefs that make our lives harder. When we're hurting, it's harder to be thoughtful and kind to people around us. Knowing this, we can empathize with others when they say hurtful things. So keep this in mind as you're dealing with people; trust that they are doing their best with their limited experiences and perspective.

ASSIGNMENT 17

Write down some things people say about your stepparenting that triggers a response in you.

ASSIGNMENT 18

When people say these things to you, what automatic thoughts or beliefs does it trigger?

ASSIGNMENT 19

Reframe your thoughts. What's a more helpful way you could think about this? (e.g., "They're saying that because they don't know how it is to be a stepparent.")

CONCLUSION

Your life as a stepparent, like the lives of other parents, can be extremely fulfilling and rewarding, however, it can also be exhausting, painful, lonely, challenging, and unhappy. Being a stepparent can bring out both the best and the worst in you. Working on your mindset empowers you to make the changes necessary for you to increase your chances of successfully blending your family: remember, the only person you can change is yourself. Throughout this workbook, if you have completed your assignments, you have engaged in deep reflection about yourself and what kind of life you want to build for yourself, your partner, and your blended family. These exercises have helped you to analyze which of your behaviors are or are not working for you and have helped to facilitate important conversations. You're off to a great start!

When you have a support network to help you navigate this role, you're much more likely to be happy and content as a stepparent. When you don't have anyone to support you, you will struggle to adapt. Fortunately, there are many support groups, therapists, or coaches available to you to help you learn what kind of stepparent you want to be and that can help you step up in that role. Don't be afraid to seek out help! Becoming a stepparent is a huge transition and one we can't prepare for by ourselves.

The key to having a happy, fulfilling life as a step-parent is making intentional decisions and reflecting on the outcome of your decisions. This can be especially difficult when you are dealing with trauma caused by your partner's past relationships, your stepchildren's emotions, insecurities, and behavior, and your own life experiences. However, if you become intentional about your life, you will be able to stay in touch with your feelings, your goals, and have a happier, better relationship with your partner and your children. The more you work on yourself and your relationship with your new blended family, the more satisfying the experience will become. Good luck to you as you co-parent your stepchildren and build a stronger, more fulfilling relationship with your partner!

APPENDICIES

Appendix A – Healthy Self-Care Activities
Appendix B – Date night ideas
Appendix C – Stepparent resources

APPENDIX A: Healthy Self-Care Activities

Coping skills can be thought of as intervention when difficult situations arise, self-care activities are prevention. Doing daily/weekly self-care is critical to our mental health as stepparents, but we also need to use coping skills when we're annoyed, frustrated, or out of control. Use the following list to help you build your list of self-care activities.

- Take a walk and pay attention to nature and your breathing.
- Exercise
- Yoga
- Hit a punching bag
- Spend time in nature
- Spend time with your friends
- Participate in meaningful family activities
- Talk to a trusted friend or family member
- Read a book
- Take care of animals or pets
- Cry
- Go Ax throwing or to a smash/rage room
- Journal
- Pray or engage in a spiritual practice
- Go to a shooting range
- Therapy
- Dance - go out or dance in your kitchen, it doesn't matter where, just let go!
- Write out your feelings then burn or tear up the paper.
- Watch a movie
- Paint/Draw
- Listen to music
- Reframe the situation
- Progressive muscle relaxation
- Guided meditation
- Get support from other stepparents
- Use problem solving strategies
- Take a bath
- Give yourself a pep talk
- Establish healthy boundaries
- Clean your house
- Find a fun or relaxing hobby
- Squeeze a stress ball
- Take a nap
- Use a relaxation app
- Look at pictures that make you happy
- Give and accept compliments
- Pay attention to your thoughts and feelings
- Identify the intensity of your emotions
- Watch a funny video
- Use positive self-talk
- Visualize your favorite place
- Eat a healthy snack
- Doodle on paper
- Do an art project
- Make a gratitude list
- Do something kind for someone else
- Play with clay or silly putty
- Garden
- Schedule time for yourself
- Write a poem
- Drink tea
- Plan a fun trip
- Ask yourself "What do I need right now?"
- Make a list of choices
- Organize a closet, drawer, or room
- Take a break
- Go for a drive
- Be assertive
- Lower your expectations of a situation
- Write a list of your strengths

Unhealthy Coping Skills

- Drinking alcohol or using drugs to escape your feelings
- Overeating
- Sleeping too much
- Repeatedly venting to others
- Acting on your feelings without giving yourself time to cool down
- Overspending/retail therapy
- Avoiding your problems
- Complaining without problem-solving
- Blaming others

My List of Self-Care Activities:

Mental

Emotional

Spiritual

APPENDIX B: Date Night Ideas

Prioritizing your relationship with your partner is vital to your happiness as a couple. These date night ideas can help you have time together to do that.

- Go to a playground and play
- See a movie
- See a play
- Take a drive
- Golf
- Have a romantic picnic
- Take a class together
- Have a game night
- Take dance lessons
- Go to a museum
- Get coffee or hot chocolate
- Volunteer together
- Have an at-home spa day
- Go bowling
- Go to a concert
- Go to a comedy show
- Watch a Netflix comedy special
- Eat spaghetti without silverware
- Go to a bookstore
- Watch the sunrise or sunset
- Visit a public garden
- Drive to see the autumn leaves
- Go to a public concert
- Rent a canoe or stand up paddleboard
- Go on a scavenger hunt
- Go out for ice cream
- Make a DIY project
- Go swimming
- Have a barbecue
- Write a silly poem
- Do a photoshoot
- Bake cookies together
- Play a new sex game
- Fly kites together
- Go through your old yearbooks or photo books
- Plan a date with a $10 limit
- Make a time capsule
- Play strip poker
- Go to open mic night
- Find a new recipe to cook together
- Play Mad Libs
- Go see a national monument
- Go frisbee golfing
- Go swimming
- Go to a lake
- Go-kart racing
- Go to an arcade
- Borrow or rent bikes
- Feed ducks at a pond
- Walk a nature trail
- Go to a public library
- Test drive a car
- Listen to old cd's, tapes, or records
- Stargaze
- Do a puzzle together
- Eat takeout by candlelight
- Play laser tag
- Go to an amusement park
- Go to a drive-in movie
- Sing at karaoke night
- Do an escape room
- Cook together
- Go wine tasting
- Do a paint night
- Do a chocolate or cheese tasting night at home
- Go to a food truck
- Go to a farmer's market
- Take a hike
- Go camping/camp at a state park
- Visit friends or a family member
- Play hide and seek

APPENDIX C: Stepparent Resources

Podcasts
Blendcredible - hosted by Tim Watson
I Know I'm Crazy - hosted by Naja Hall
Stepping Forward Podcast - hosted by Sara Susov and Rachel Rawlinson
The Essential Stepmom - hosted by Tracy Poizner
The Jamie Scrimgeour Podcast
The Stepmom Club - hosted by Grady Savage
The Step-mom Strong Podcast - hosted by Nathalie Savell

Books
The Empowered Stepmom - Tuniscia O

The Single Girl's Guide to Marrying a Man, His Kids, and His Ex-wife:
Becoming a Step-mom with Humor and Grace - Sally Bjornsen

The Stepmoms Club - Kendall Rose

Stepmom Magazine - edited by Brenda Ockun
https://www.facebook.com/StepMomMagazine

Facebook Groups/Pages
Sara Susov - Step Up Mentoring
https://www.facebook.com/stepupmentoring

Step Up to Stepparenting
https://www.facebook.com/groups/stepupmentoring/

The Spectacular Stepmom
https://www.facebook.com/groups/thespectacularstepmom/

Blended and Black
https://www.facebook.com/groups/BlendedandBlack/

Bonus Mom Without My Own
(good for stepmoms with no bio kids)
https://www.facebook.com/groups/190867244731559/

Not Just a Stepmom - Heidi Farrell
https://www.facebook.com/notjuststepmom

Conferences
Stepmoms Alive
https://www.facebook.com/StepMomsALIVE/

The Smart Stepmom Retreat - Laura Petherbridge
https://www.facebook.com/The-Smart-Stepmom-1849483092049217

The Stepmom Connection
https://www.facebook.com/stepmomconnection

Stepfamily Events
https://www.facebook.com/stepfamilyevents

Printed in the USA
CPSIA information can be obtained
at www.ICGtesting.com
LVHW080422291124
797659LV00006B/73